Weight Loss after Pregnancy

Tarla Dalal
INDIA'S #1 COOKERY AUTHOR

S&C
SANJAY & CO.
MUMBAI

COOK BOOKS BY TARLA DALAL

INDIAN COOKING
- Tava Cooking
- Rotis & Subzis
- Desi Khana
- The Complete Gujarati Cook Book
- Mithai
- Chaat
- Achaar aur Parathe
- The Rajasthani Cookbook
- Swadisht Subzian
- Punjabi Khana New
- Mughlai Khana New
- South Indian Recipes New

WESTERN COOKING
- The Complete Italian Cookbook
- The Chocolate Cookbook
- Eggless Desserts
- Mocktails & Snacks
- Thai Cooking
- Soups & Salads
- Mexican Cooking
- Chinese Cooking
- Easy Chinese Cooking
- Sizzlers & Barbeques
- Cakes & Pastries New
- Party Drinks New
- Wraps & Rolls New

MINI SERIES
- Cooking Under 10 minutes
- Pizzas and Pasta
- Fun Food for Children
- Roz ka Khana
- Idlis & Dosas
- Microwave - Desi Khana
- Paneer
- Parathas
- Chawal
- Dals
- Sandwiches
- Quick Cooking
- Curries & Kadhis
- Chinese Recipes
- Jain Desi Khana
- 7 Dinner Menus
- Jain International Recipes
- Punjabi Subzis
- Chips & dips
- Corn
- Microwave Subzis
- Baked Dishes
- Stir-Fry
- Potatoes
- Recipes Using Leftovers
- Noodles
- Lebenese
- Cook Book for Two's
- Know your Dals & Pulses
- Fruit & Vegetable Carving
- Know your Spices
- Know your Flours
- Popular Restaurant Gravies
- Paneer Snacks New
- Know Your Green Leafy Vegetables New
- Pressure Cooker Recipes New

TOTAL HEALTH
- Low Calorie Healthy Cooking
- Pregnancy Cookbook
- Baby and Toddler Cookbook
- Cooking with 1 Teaspoon of Oil
- Home Remedies
- Delicious Diabetic Recipes
- Fast Foods Made Healthy
- Healthy Soups & Salads
- Healthy Breakfast
- Calcium Rich Recipes
- Healthy Heart Cook Book
- Forever Young Diet
- Healthy Snacks
- Iron Rich Recipes
- Healthy Juices
- Low Cholesterol Recipes
- Good Food for Diabetes
- Healthy Subzis
- Healthy Snacks for Kids
- High Blood Pressure Cook Book
- Low Calorie Sweets
- Nutritious Recipes for Pregnancy
- Diabetic Snacks
- Zero Oil Rotis & Subzis
- Zero Oil Soups, Salads & Snacks
- Zero Oil Dal & Chawal
- Acidity Cook Book
- Growing Kids Cookbook
- Soya Rotis & Subzis
- Cooking with Sprouts
- Exotic Diabetic Cooking - Part 1
- Healthy Diabetic Cooking
- Protein Rich Recipes New
- Eat Well Stay Well New
- Weight Loss After Pregnancy New
- 100 Calories Snacks New

GENERAL COOKING
- Exciting Vegetarian Cooking
- Microwave Recipes
- Saatvik Khana
- The Pleasures of Vegetarian Cooking
- The Delights of Vegetarian Cooking
- The Joys of Vegetarian Cooking
- Cooking with Kids
- Snacks Under 10 Minutes
- Ice-Cream & Frozen Desserts
- Desserts Under 10 Minutes
- Entertaining
- Microwave Snacks & Desserts
- Kebabs & Tikkis New
- Non-fried Snacks New

First Printing : 2009

Copyright © Sanjay & Co.

ISBN : 978-81-89491-64-2

Price Rs. 250/-

Published & Distributed by :
SANJAY & COMPANY
353/A-1, Shah & Nahar Industrial Estate, Dhanraj Mill Compound, Lower Parel (W), Mumbai - 400 013. INDIA.
Tel. : (91-22) 4345 2400 • Fax : (91-22) 2496 5876 • E-mail : sanjay@tarladalal.com • Website : www.tarladalal.com

"Tarla Dalal" is also a registered trademark owned by Sanjay & Co.

ALL RIGHTS RESERVED WITH THE PUBLISHERS.
No portion of this book shall be reproduced, stored in retrieval system or transmitted by any means, electronic, mechanical, photocopying, recording or otherwise, without the written permission of the publishers.

Disclaimer : While every precaution has been taken in the preparation of this book, the publishers and the author assume no responsibility for errors or omissions. Neither is any liability assumed for damages resulting from the use of information contained herein.

Bulk Purchases : Tarla Dalal Cookbooks are ideal gifts. If you are interested in buying more than 500 assorted copies of Tarla Dalal Cookbooks at special prices, please contact us at 91-22-4345 2400 or email : sanjay@tarladalal.com

---

UK and USA customers can call us on :
UK : 02080029533   •   USA : 213-634-1406
For books, Membership on tarladalal.com, Subscription for **Cooking & More** and Recipe queries
Timing : 9.30 a.m. to 7.00 p.m. (IST), from Monday to Saturday
Local call charges applicable

Recipe Research, & Production Design
Sapna Kamdar
Brinda Gandhi

Nutritionist
Nisha Katira

Photography / Food Stylist
Payal Choksi / Arati Fedane
page 27, 32, 34, 45, 49, 57, 71, 73, 77, 79 & 92

Copy Editor
Roli Gupta

Design
Vinod Patil

Weight Management & Yoga Consultant
Deepti Bansal Seth

Printed by
Minal Sales Agencies, Mumbai

INTRODUCTION

Having a baby is undoubtedly the most wonderful experience for any woman…At once challenging and joyful; motherhood brings with it a whirlwind of activity and parental responsibility – making the new mother so busy that she often forgets to look after her overall health. Weight gain during the gestation period is unavoidable and unfortunately going back to the slim, pre-pregnancy shape is difficult. There is a plethora of questions that confuse the young mother in her quest to lose weight - When can I start the weight loss programme?, Will it affect my baby?, Which is the best exercise to tone up the muscles?, What is the best diet for me?, and so on…

My book **"WEIGHT LOSS AFTER PREGNANCY"** is your guide to coming out of this entire dilemma. A sequel to the existing **"Pregnancy Cookbook"** and **"Baby and Toddler Cookbook"**, this book is aimed at helping new mothers shed the excess weight in a healthy manner. With growing evidence of increased risk of developing diabetes and cardio vascular disease in later life, losing weight in a healthy manner is more essential than merely fulfilling the new mother's desire to look slim.

This book keeps in mind the special nutrient requirements of the lactating mothers. Moreover, it also provides step by step instructions and illustrations of various exercises and yogasanas for a holistic approach to weight loss.

This book follows the main principle of – "Lose the fats, not the nutrients"

60 delectable recipes cover all the major 6 courses viz. **Breakfast (like Stuffed Wheat Dosa, page 22, Banana and Apple Porridge, page 25 etc.), Soups and Salads (like Nourishing Moong Soup, page 31, Citrus Salad, page 39 etc.), Snacks (like Poha and Oats Chivda, page 47, Soya Sesame Khakhras, page 50 etc.), Rotis and Subzis (like Carrot and Bean Sprout Paratha, page 60, Soya Bhurji, page 63 etc.), Rice and Dal (like Tendli Bhaat, page 68, Subzi Kadhi, page 83 etc.) and Desserts (like Sugar-free Date Rolls, page 88, Oats and Orange Rabadi, page 89 etc.).** With such a wide range, lactating mothers will find it easy to plan complete tasty and nutrient-rich meals for themselves and at the same time ward off potential health risks.

Go ahead…I am sure that the postpartum weight loss will be a pleasant journey with this book to assist you.

Here's wishing all the new mothers a happy and healthy weight loss!

Regards

Tarla Dalal

INDEX

- Introduction 6
- Why is Weight Loss after Pregnancy Important? 6
- When Should the Postpartum Weight Loss Program be Started? 6
- Theories of Weight Loss 6
- Factors Affecting Weight Loss 7
- Yoga & Weight Loss 11

Breakfast 17

- Spicy Chapati Rolls 18
- Ami Kozhakatai 19
- Dal and Vegetable Handvo 20
- Stuffed Wheat Dosa 22
- Semiyan Upma 24
- Banana and Apple Porridge 25
- Cottage Cheese and Dill Canapés 26
- Soya Poha 27
- Muesli 28

Soups and Salads 29

- Garlic Vegetable Soup 30
- Nourishing Moong Soup 31
- Carrot and Coriander Soup 32
- Green Pea Soup 33
- Hot Borscht 34
- Spicy Stir-Fry Soup 35
- Dalia and Vegetable Salad 36
- Sprouts and Vegetable Salad 37
- Summer Salad 38
- Citrus Salad 39
- Fruity Sprouts Salad 40

Snacks 41

- Stuffed Spinach Pancakes 42
- Masala Chana 44
- Dry Figs and Banana Smoothie 45
- Mini Sprouts Uttapa 46
- Poha and Oats Chivda 47
- Hariyali Chanki 48
- Soya Sesame Khakhra 50
- Pineapple Stir-Fry 51
- Club Sandwich 52
- Watermelon Apple Drink 54

Roti and Subzi 55

- Suva Chawal Roti..56
- Garlic Roti..57
- Soya Toovar Dal Roti...................................58
- Chilkewale Parathe.......................................59
- Paneer, Carrot and Bean Sprouts Paratha.......60
- Ridge Gourd with Poppy Seeds...................62
- Soya Bhurji...63
- Rajma Saagwala...64
- Baby Corn Paneer Jalfraize..........................66

Rice and Dal 67

- Tendli Bhaat 68
- Ram Khichdi...70
- Vegetable Pulao 72
- Tava Sprouts Pulao.......................................74
- Bengali Khichdi..76
- Hare Lehsun Ki Dal 78
- Suva Masoor Dal...80
- Methiche Varan 81
- Dapka Kadhi 82
- Subzi Kadhi 83
- Jeera Pepper Rasam......................................84

Desserts 85

- Healthy Sheera..86
- Rose Barfi...87
- Sugar-free Date Rolls...................................88
- Oats and Orange Rabadi...............................89
- Poha Phirni...90
- Fruit Bowl with Vanilla Cream.....................91
- Anjeer Basundi..92

Basic Recipes 93

- Low-Fat Curds 94
- Low-Fat Hung Curds 94
- Paneer / Low-Fat Paneer 95
- Low-Fat Mava 96

INTRODUCTION

Congratulations for the new bundle of joy that's now such an inseparable part of your life. From the time you've known that you are pregnant to the time that the child was delivered, a whole lot of advice on all sorts of topics from food to baby care must have poured in from all sources. But the kind of care that is needed post-delivery is a completely different ball game. With so much advice and so many tips, I am sure there must be a lot of confusion between what's right and what's wrong. I too had a similar phase – there was a roller coaster of emotions, where I was happy, confused, anxious and at a complete loss to understand how to go about this new life. One important thing that I realized was that the new responsibility is so overwhelming for you as a mother that you forget to take care of yourself!

The postpartum period is a difficult time – though you are out of your pregnant state, your body is still sore from the whole process of pregnancy and delivery. Additionally, the newborn has to be nursed and cared for. You long to come back to your original pre-pregnancy weight, which unfortunately is not an immediate process, and requires tremendous patience, time and effort.

WHY IS WEIGHT LOSS AFTER PREGNANCY IMPORTANT?

Weight loss after pregnancy is essential to reduce the risk of developing diabetes and cardiovascular disease later in life. In fact, women who become overweight during pregnancy and are unable to shed off excess fat within a period of six months after the delivery, have an elevated risk of becoming obese a decade later.

WHEN SHOULD THE POSTPARTUM WEIGHT LOSS PROGRAM BE STARTED?

Once the baby has been delivered, the top priority for most of the mothers is to get back their pre-pregnancy shape and get into their old clothes. However, one should not start a weight loss program immediately after pregnancy. Since the baby is breastfeeding, you cannot compromise on your food intake by cutting down on your diet, nor can you immediately start off on rigorous exercise. The weight loss program must begin in a slow and phased manner – simple exercises initially, followed by rigorous work-outs much later, once the baby is weaned. Adequate nutrition is essential all along, and cannot be compromised at any time. It's preferable to start a weight loss program only after 6 weeks. Those who have had a caesarean section must wait until 8 weeks till they have recovered from the surgery to embark upon a weight loss program. The pattern of weight loss after pregnancy varies with each mother but the greatest amount of weight loss occurs in the first 3 months postpartum and then continues at a slow and steady rate until 6 months postpartum. It's common to put on or retain the pregnancy weight. Disheartenment and guilt at not being able to lose weight is common. But, where it took 9 months to gain weight, it is natural that another 9 months or even more would be needed to lose it. Patience therefore is the key to keep going!

THEORIES OF WEIGHT LOSS
1. Lipolysis
Lipolysis is the process that results in freeing fats from their fat stores in the body, and thus

contributes to weight loss. When the sugar level in the blood is low, the insulin levels are also low. Therefore, to make up for the demand of energy, fat is released from the fat deposits of the body and weight loss occurs.

2. Calorie Theory

Energy is needed to meet the various requirements of body:
- Basal functions- Maintenance of body temperature, functioning of various organs, digestion, wear and tear of tissues.
- Physical activity.

The energy requirement of every individual varies and is based on lifestyle, sex, health status and metabolism.

If an individual needs 2600 kcal a day and consumes only 2000 kcal, there is a resultant deficit of 600 kcal. To compensate for this, the body draws calories from the fat reserves and weight loss will result by the process of lipolysis. On the other hand, if the intake is more than requirement, extra calories will be stored as body fat.

FACTORS AFFECTING WEIGHT LOSS

The most important factors affecting weight loss during the postnatal period are **breastfeeding, consuming a proper, balanced diet** and **regular exercise**. These factors are briefly described below:

Breastfeeding

It is a well-acknowledged fact that breastfeeding not only helps in postpartum weight loss, but also provides important benefits such as reduced risk of breast and ovarian cancer, decreased risk of hip fractures and a natural contraception aiding in adequate birth spacing.

Breastfeeding assists weight loss, if continued for 12 months after delivery. The process of breastfeeding releases a number of hormones, which help the uterus to return to its pre-pregnancy size and shape. However don't depend only on breastfeeding to lose weight. You still have to be careful about the diet, otherwise you may gain weight instead of losing it. If you are breastfeeding there is no reason why you should not go on a healthy, low-fat weight loss diet, but do not drop your energy intake below 1800 calories per day. So be sure to eat sensibly, exercise regularly and allow nature to do the rest.

Diet

Indian culture in the name of postnatal care causes a lot of weight problems for the lactating mother. You are made to eat a lot of fatty foods, like ghee and nuts-laden sweets, rest all day, is not allowed to exercise. This not only makes you fat and lazy, but it also causes depression, which could lead to eating disorders.

Keeping in mind the nutrient needs for the lactating mother we have prepared the following guidelines that will ensure that you eat healthy while having enough calories and nutrients.

A. Slow and steady wins the race

- Avoid losing weight using drastic measures. Fad diets will show results in the short run. However, in the long run you will end up craving for foods that had been in the restricted list and thereby end up piling more weight than before. Balance and moderation is the key to a healthy and effective weight loss program. Patience is the key to slow and steady weight loss.
- Be realistic about your weight loss program. A weight loss of 0.5 to 1 kg per week is scientifically sound and achievable. Remember you are modifying habits and making lifelong changes.

B. Tweak your cooking style

- Steam, stir-fry or microwave food. For great taste just spice them up with herbs, spices, lemon juice or vinegar. Presenting the food tastefully using variety of garnishes and colourful vegetables will make the food appealing.
- Use non-stick cookware to cook food to reduce the amount of oil used in cooking. It's preferable to bake rather than deep-fry certain snacks and *farsan*.
- Always use oil sparingly while cooking. If a recipe calls for 1 teaspoon of oil, measure it rather than guessing.
- Replace full fat dairy products with low-fat alternatives like low-fat milk, curds and *paneer* and skim milk powder.
- Use low-fat salad dressings instead of mayonnaise and salad cream. Try the recipe of **Citrus Salad, page 39 and Fruity Sprouts Salad, page 40**.
- Instead of coconut and cashewnuts, use vegetable purées in gravies or opt for tomato based gravies.

C. Eat the right way

- Eat a variety of foods, but in moderation. Your body needs more than 40 different nutrients to stay healthy. Preferably eat foods that are low in calories and aid in milk production also known as galactogogues.
- Choose whole wheat products or multi-grain products like breads, *khakhras* etc. to increase your fibre intake. Avoid refined flour and its products as they are not a good source of fibre and nutrients.
- Avoid foods that are fried or extremely fatty. They provide unnecessary amount of calories, which add to weight gain. It is better to stick to healthy and nutritious food.
- Drink enough fluids, but not too much. Between 2 – 3 litres a day is a good goal to aim for. Some mothers discover they need much more, and some find that they need to get "just enough" fluids to maintain an optimal milk supply. Liquids can be in the form of plain water, soups, fruit and vegetable juices, low-fat milk etc.
- Eat at least one warm meal per day that includes a source of protein such as *dal* or low-fat curds, sprouts, low-fat *paneer* etc.
- Stop snacking on peanuts, almonds and other nuts as these have plenty of hidden fats. Rather snack on healthy foods like dried *chana*, or *sukha bhel*, but avoid adding *sev* and *puri* to it.

- Avoid having sugar-laden juices and carbonated beverages as they only add provide empty calories without being a significant source of nutrients. Stick to fresh fruit and vegetable juices to quench your thirst. However, whole fruits and vegetables are a better alternative to juices as they contain fibre which helps detoxify the body.
- Have herbs that rebuild the blood lost during birth. Some spices like turmeric help prevent breast inflammation. Include spices like black pepper, *ajwain* and fennel that help in relieving flatulence and prevent gas formation in the daily diet. Make *mukhwas* using fennel, *ajwain*, dry coconut or use turmeric and pepper to flavour your foods.

D. Change your eating pattern

- Keep the meals simple and savour your meals. With the added responsibility of raising a child, it is essential that the meals you prepare are simple yet wholesome. Elaborate meals are difficult to digest in the initial days and will take too much time to prepare, leaving you with no time for yourself and for essential exercises.
- Eat slowly! It gives your brain a chance to send the 'I'm full' signal to your stomach before you overeat.
- Avoid eating to the point that you are stuffed and you can't eat any further. Have just enough till the point that you feel satisfied and full.
- Avoid serving yourself huge portions of food. If you feel hungry after completion of one portion then you can serve yourself another portion.
- If you are in the mood of having something sweet always share your dessert or simply have some of the sugar-free desserts, dates or fruits freely available in the market. Please ensure that they are low-fat too.

Physical Activity

To lose weight, you must burn more calories than you consume. This can be achieved by increasing your activity, not by drastically reducing your calorie intake. Reduction of calories intake causes the metabolism to slow down, defeating the very purpose of your entire weight loss program. Regular exercise, even if it is only dancing with your baby to music or taking her out for walks, is the best approach.

A few mothers are worried that regular and sustained, moderate-to-high intensity exercise will impair the quality or quantity of breast milk. Exercise may sometimes increase the lactic acid concentration in breast milk, making it sour, which causes the baby to decrease suckling. However, such cases are very rare. Feeding the baby prior to exercise should negate any potential problem, as any lactic acid that does accumulate in the breast milk generally clears up in 30 to 60 minutes post-exercise. The mother can alternatively express milk in a bottle and then feed it to the child once she finishes the exercises.

- ### The many benefits of exercise

1. Losing your pregnancy weight is not the only benefit of postpartum exercise. Just like antenatal exercises, postnatal fitness helps ease a host of discomforts simply by increasing the blood circulation.
2. Exercise can also help with any postpartum depression you might be experiencing.
3. If you maintain your exercise regime, you will be providing your children with an excellent example of how to stay healthy.

4. Exercise improves cardiovascular fitness, plasma lipids, and insulin response in lactating women. However, exercise alone without caloric restriction does not promote weight loss. Once lactation is established, over-weight women may restrict their energy intake by 500 calories/day to promote weight loss of 0.5 kg/week without affecting the growth of the infant.

Note: To maximize the benefits of your exercise, try to stick to a well-balanced, healthy diet. And remember, whenever you work out, always drink plenty of water. Warm-up and cool-down properly and never exercise to the point of exhaustion.

- ### When can I start exercising?

If you've had a normal delivery then you can start exercising 6 weeks after your baby's birth. However, if you've had a cesarean section allow yourself 8 weeks time to recover from the surgery before you set out to exercise. However, you are the best judge and know best when you are ready to start exercising.

- ### Start stretching right away

If you've had a safe and healthy delivery, you can start stretching your legs right away to loosen your leg muscles. Start out with some kegel exercises that involve contraction of vaginal muscles, which will help in the contraction of the uterine muscles. All you need to do is simply contract these muscles the same way that you control the urge to pass urine. Hold the contraction for 20-30 seconds and gradually release the muscles.

- ### Stick to a routine

Ensure that you have a well-chalked out routine for yourself that will help you stick to your exercise plan. You can take your baby in a sling bag or in a pram when you want to go out for a walk. If there are other new mothers in the vicinity you can form a group and go for a walk together. In this manner your child can be taken care of by other mothers too, making your routine lively and interesting.

- ### Simple tips for exercising

✓ **Walking:** is a fun and simple way to keep fit. Going outdoors for a walk helps rejuvenate, take in some fresh air and also helps loosen up leg muscles. People who are prone to post-pregnancy depression will see their mood change for the better. The zest to lead life well and enjoy motherhood improves substantially.

✓ **Gym Workout:** Signing up to a gym is another great way to shed those extra pounds and return to pre-pregnancy weight. By performing both cardio and weight bearing exercises one is assured of losing weight as well toning the muscles. It also strengthens bones and prevents osteoporosis. However, it is essential to perform these exercises under the supervision of a trained instructor to prevent injury.

✓ **Swimming:** This is a great cardiovascular exercise which helps in building stamina.

✓ **Yoga:** Some mothers prefer learning yoga and doing it within the comfort of the home rather than going out for a full fledged workout. Yoga is a great way to tone muscles and improve mental as well as physical well-being. Yoga is helpful not only for weight loss, but also helps in relaxing the body and mind, thus enabling the woman to maintain good physical and mental health.

YOGA & WEIGHT LOSS

It is necessary to introduce exercise into your new routine to allow your muscles to return to their former length, strength and functional capability. Exercise also tones the body and knocks off unwanted fat.

Many women want to resume intense exercise as soon as possible, before their abdominal muscles or pelvic muscles are ready. This may lead to incontinence problems and prolonged back pain. You can start light yogic *asanas* and breathing exercises, as early as 24-48 hours after birth. You should not approach your exercises in a strenuous manner, but rather do them lightly and regularly. A complete yogic workout can be started after a minimum of 6 weeks post-delivery.

Points to keep in mind while performing yoga:

1. It is ideal to do the workout twice daily – morning and evening.
2. Perform the *asanas* on an empty stomach or 3 hours after the meals.
3. As a beginner do not attempt to do more than 1 repetition of each *asana*. Later, with practice you could go to 2 to 3 repetitions of each *asana* and also increase the holding period.
4. Wear comfortable clothing while performing *asanas*.
5. When holding any *asana*, make sure that there is no discomfort, if any discomfort occurs, release the *asana*.
6. Concentration on maintaining a slow rhythmic, sustaining breath while performing any *asana* is very important.

ASANAS

Below are a set of *asanas* and breathing exercises. Coupled with a healthy diet, they work very well to help achieve your target weight loss. Before beginning the yoga routine, it is a must to perform the basic breathing exercise - Diaphragmatic Breathing.

Diaphragmatic Breathing

Benefit: The elongated and flabby muscles in the belly are toned. When performed with proper exercises, the fat around the stomach gets reduced.

One of the best and easy ways to start toning the abdominal muscles is by using them in conscious breathing exercises.

1. Lie down on the mat with legs bent at the knees.
2. Place one palm on the navel area and the other palm on the mat facing downwards.
3. Slowly inhale from the nose and feel the stomach expand.
4. Slowly exhale from the nose and feel the abdomen area flatten.
5. Repeat this 10 to 15 times.

ASANA SEQUENCE FOR THE UPPER BODY
Parvatasana (Mountain pose)

Benefit: Helps to reduce fat from the belly and arms.

1. Sit in *padmasana* / *sukhasana* (with simple crossed leg).

2. Gently inhale, join both your palms in a *namaste* position and raise them above your head keeping the elbows straight. Your biceps should be ideally touching your ears. Stretch your hands upwards towards the ceiling as high as you can all the while remaining in contact with the floor. Do not interlock your thumbs. Breathe normally and remain in this position for 5 to 10 seconds. The holding time can be stretched up to 2 minutes later.

3. Gently exhale and return to the original position.

Variation I

From step 2, inhale gently and twist your upper body towards your left side without moving the lower body. Breathe normally and remain in this position for 5 to 10 seconds. Exhale gently and return to the centre position. Perform the same step on your right side.

Variation II

From step 2, inhale gently and bend your upper body towards your left side without moving the lower body. Breathe normally and remain in this position for 5 to 10 seconds. Exhale gently and return to the centre position. Perform the same step on your right side.

Variation III

From step 2, inhale gently and bend your upper body backwards without moving the lower body. Breathe normally and remain in this position for 5 to10 seconds. Exhale gently and return to the centre position.

Exhale gently and bend your upper body forward with hands parallel to the floor. Breathe normally and remain in this position for 5 to10 seconds. Inhale gently and return to the centre position.

Hastapadasana (Forward Bend Pose)

Benefit: Helps in toning the abdominal area.

1. Stand straight with head, back and neck in one line, arms by your side and the feet placed one foot distance apart.

2. Inhale gently, raise both your arms straight up and bend backwards slightly.

3. Exhale gently, bend forward starting first from your waist, then your neck and finally your head. Try to hold your ankles and bring the forehead close to the knees. Breathe normally and remain in this position for 5 to 10 seconds.

4. Inhale gently, raise the hands and head upward together and while exhaling gently bring the hands down.

Naukasana (Boat pose)

Benefit: Strengthens the core muscles, thus reducing flabbiness near the abdomen.

1. Lie down on a mat with legs together and arms facing downwards close to the thighs and inhale in this position.

2. While exhaling, slowly raise both the hands and legs and back above the floor at a 45° angle without bending the knees and the elbows. Breathe normally and remain in this position for 5 to 10 seconds.

3. Gently exhale and rest the hands, legs and back to the floor.

Yoga Mudra

Benefit: Helps in toning the stomach and shoulder areas.

1. Sit in *padmasana/sukhasana*.

2. Hold the wrist of one hand by the other from behind. Gently inhale and press the shoulders slightly backwards.

3. Exhale gently and bend forward to touch the floor. Relax shoulders when bending down. (If touching the floor is not possible, bend as much as you can). Breathe normally and remain in this position for 5 to 10 seconds.

4. Inhale gently and come up to the original position and relax.

ASANA SEQUENCE FOR THE LOWER BODY

Utkatasana (Squatting Pose)

Benefit: Helps toning the calf muscles and strengthen the knees.

1. Stand straight with the head, back and neck in one line, arms by your side and the feet placed one foot (6") distance apart.

2. Breathe in deeply and slowly bring the hands straight up so that the palms and shoulders are in one straight line, simultaneously raise the heels above the floor.

3. Exhale gently and lower yourself towards the ground by bending your knees slightly downwards (that is, squat) while keeping your back straight and your heels raised. Breathe normally and remain in this position for 5 to 10 seconds.

4. Inhale gently and again come up straight and while exhaling bring the palms down next to the thigh and heels on the floor.

Virabhadrasana III (Warrior Pose III)

Benefit: Helps in toning the thigh muscles and improve body balance.

1. Stand straight with the head, back and neck in one straight line. Focus at a point straight in front, to improve body balance in this *asana*.

1. Inhale normally and while exhaling raise the left leg perpendicular to the floor up and simultaneously lower the torso forward and spread the arms.

2. The palm and shoulders should be in one straight line and the trunk (upper body) parallel to the floor. The right leg should be completely straight. Breathe normally and remain in this position for 4 to 5 seconds.

3. Inhale slowly, bringing the leg down and return to position 1.

Adho Mukha Svanasana (Downward Facing Dog Pose)

Benefit: Helps in toning the legs.

1. Sit on the mat on your hands and knees with your palms spread shoulder-width apart and feet one foot (6") apart.

2. Exhale gently and lift the knees above the floor and draw the back and pelvic area upwards towards the ceiling. Keep the arms straight with the palms firmly pressed onto the floor, and head facing inwards towards the knees. Heels should touch the floor to get maximum stretch on the legs. Breathe normally and remain in this position for 15 seconds.

3. Inhale gently and rest your knees on the floor and come back to step 1 position.

Breakfast

Spicy Chapati Rolls

Preparation Time: 20 minutes.   Cooking Time: 5 to 7 minutes.   Makes 4 rolls.

Save time while retaining the taste and nutrition that this spicy dish made from left-tover chapatis provide. Fibre rich baby corn and capsicum in the stuffing aid weight loss.

For the stuffing
2 tsp oil
¼ cup sliced onions
½ cup boiled, peeled and grated potatoes
4 to 6 baby corn, sliced
½ cup coloured capsicum (red, yellow and green) cubes
2 tsp roasted peanuts, crushed
½ tsp chilli powder
½ tsp *garam masala*
1 seasoning cube (vegetarian), optional
1 tbsp lemon juice
Salt to taste

Other ingredients
4 whole wheat *chapatis* [approx. 150 mm. (6") in diameter]

For the stuffing
1. Heat the oil in a non-stick pan, add the onions and sauté on a medium flame for 2 to 3 minutes or till they turn translucent.
2. Add all the remaining ingredients, mix well and cook on a medium flame for 2 minutes. Keep aside.

How to proceed
1. Warm a *chapati* lightly on a non-stick *tava* (griddle).
2. Remove on a plate, place ¼ of the stuffing on one side of the *chapati* and roll it up tightly.
3. Repeat with the remaining *chapatis* and stuffing to make 3 more rolls.
   Serve immediately.

Nutritive values per roll
Energy	: 84 calories
Protein	: 2.0 gm
Carbohydrates	: 11.8 gm
Fat	: 3.6 gm
Vitamin C	**: 20.2 mg**
Fibre	**: 1.0 gm**

Ami Kozhakatai

Preparation Time: 10 minutes.   Cooking Time: 20 minutes.   Serves 4.

Delicately seasoned with simple spices, this is one dish that you will relish. I have added only 1 tsp of coconut to bring down the calories, making this a sumptuous, healthy breakfast when compared to the coconut laden South Indian original.

1¼ cups rice flour (*chawal ka atta*)
½ tsp salt
1¾ tsp oil for greasing and tempering
1 tsp mustard seeds (*rai / sarson*)
1 tsp *urad dal* (split black lentils)
2 whole dry Kashmiri red chillies, broken into pieces
A pinch of asafoetida (*hing*)
8 to 10 curry leaves (*kadi patta*)

For the garnish
1 tsp freshly grated coconut (optional)
1 tbsp finely chopped coriander (*dhania*)

1. Combine the rice flour, salt and 1¾ cups of water in a bowl and mix well to make a smooth batter of pouring consistency.
2. Grease a non-stick *kadhai* using ¼ tsp of oil, pour the batter in it and cook on a medium flame, while stirring continuously till it leaves the sides of the *kadhai* and resembles a dough. Keep aside.
3. Remove on a greased *thali* and knead (while hot) using ¼ tsp of oil till smooth.
4. Cover the dough with a wet muslin cloth and keep aside for 5 minutes.
5. Rub ¼ tsp of oil on your hands, divide the dough into 35 to 40 equal portions (small) and shape each into a round ball. Steam in an *idli* steamer for 5 to 7 minutes. Keep aside.
6. Heat the remaining 1 tsp of oil in another non-stick *kadhai* and add the mustard seeds.
7. When the seeds crackle, add the *urad dal*, red chillies, asafoetida and curry leaves and sauté on a medium flame for a few seconds.
8. Add the steamed rice balls, toss well and cook on a medium flame for another minute,
Serve hot garnished with coconut and coriander.

Nutritive values per serving	
Energy	: 161 calories
Protein	: 2.9 gm
Carbohydrates	: 30.1 gm
Fat	: 3.2 gm

Dal and Vegetable Handvo

Preparation Time: 15 minutes. **Cooking Time:** 20 minutes. **Serves 4.**

This high protein variation of the traditional Gujarati savory cake uses moong dal and semolina. Rich in folic acid, iron and zinc, this is a tasty way to speed up red blood cell development to make up for blood loss after delivery. I've cooked this in a non-stick pan to minimize oil usage.

1 cup yellow *moong dal* (split yellow gram) paste, refer handy tip
3 tbsp semolina (*rawa / sooji*)
½ cup grated bottle gourd (*doodhi/ lauki*)
¼ cup grated carrots
2 tbsp finely chopped coriander (*dhania*)
1 tbsp crushed garlic (*lehsun*), optional
½ tsp turmeric powder (*haldi*)
¼ tsp chilli powder
2 tsp sugar
2 tsp lemon juice
½ tsp ginger-green chilli paste
Salt to taste
2 tsp oil
1 tsp mustard seeds (*rai/ sarson*)
1 tsp sesame seeds (*til*)
½ tsp asafoetida (*hing*)
2 tsp fruit salt

1. Combine the *moong dal* paste, semolina, bottle gourd, carrots, coriander, garlic, turmeric powder, chilli powder, sugar, lemon juice, ginger-green chilli paste and salt in a bowl and mix well to make a batter.
2. Divide the batter into 2 equal portions.
3. Sprinkle the fruit salt on 1 portion of the batter. and add 2 tsp of water over it.
4. When the bubbles form, mix gently.
5. Meanwhile, heat 1 tsp of oil in a non-stick *kadhai* and add ¼ tsp of mustard seeds.
6. When the seeds crackle, add ½ tsp of sesame seeds and ¼ tsp of asafoetida and sauté on a medium flame for a few seconds.
7. Pour the batter and spread it evenly to make a thick layer.
8. Cover and cook on a slow flame for 7 to 8 minutes or till the base turns golden brown in colour and crisp.
9. Lift the *handvo* gently using 2 large flat spoons and turn it over to the other side.
10. Cover and cook on a slow flame for another 5 to 7 minutes or till it turns golden brown in colour.
11. Cool slightly and cut it into equal pieces.
12. Repeat with the remaining portion to make 1 more *handvo*.
    Serve immediately.

Handy tip: To get 1 cup of yellow *moong dal* paste, clean, wash and soak ½ cup of yellow *moong dal* in enough water for 3 to 4 hours. Drain and blend in a mixer to a smooth paste.

Nutritive values per serving

Energy	: 134 calories
Protein	**: 5.7 gm**
Carbohydrates	: 21.4 gm
Fat	: 2.0 gm
Iron	**: 1.0 mg**
Zinc	**: 0.6 mg**
Folic Acid	**: 27.1 mg**

Stuffed Wheat Dosa

Preparation Time: 10 minutes. Cooking Time: 30 minutes. Makes 8 *dosas*.
Soaking time: ½ hour.

This unique wheat dosa is enriched with urad dal, rice flour and chana dal. Tempered with simple spices, the flavourful low-fat paneer and green peas stuffing provides essential protein, iron and fibre without the excess calories and fat.

For the *dosa* batter
1 cup whole wheat flour (*gehun ka atta*)
1 tbsp rice flour (*chawal ka atta*)
½ tsp oil
1 tsp *chana dal* (split Bengal gram), soaked for ½ hour and drained
½ tsp *urad dal* (split black lentil), soaked for ½ hour and drained
¼ tsp mustard seeds (*rai / sarson*)
¼ tsp cumin seeds (*jeera*)
5 to 6 curry leaves (*kadi patta*)
1 tsp finely chopped green chillies
Salt to taste
¼ tsp fruit salt

For the stuffing
½ tsp oil
½ tsp cumin seeds (*jeera*)
1 green chilli, finely chopped
¼ cup chopped tomatoes
1 cup boiled green peas
½ cup diced low-fat *paneer* (cottage cheese), page 95
1 tsp *chaat masala*
2 tbsp finely chopped coriander (*dhania*)
Salt to taste

Other ingredients
2¼ tsp oil for greasing and cooking

For the *dosa* batter
1. Combine the wheat flour and rice flour in a bowl, add enough water and mix well to make a smooth batter. Keep aside.
2. For the tempering, heat the oil in a small non-stick pan and add the *chana dal*, *urad dal*, mustard seeds and cumin seeds.
3. When the seeds crackle, add the curry leaves and green chillies, pour this tempering over the *dosa* batter and mix well. Keep aside.

For the stuffing
1. Heat the oil in a non-stick pan and add the cumin seeds.
2. When the seeds crackle, add the green chillies and tomatoes, mix well and sauté on a medium flame for 2 to 3 minutes.
3. Add the green peas, *paneer*, *chaat masala*, coriander and salt, mix well and sauté on a medium flame for another minute.
4. Divide the stuffing into 8 equal portions and keep aside.

How to proceed
1. Add the fruit salt to the *dosa* batter and sprinkle a few drops of water over it.
2. When the bubbles form, mix gently.
3. Heat a non-stick *tava* (griddle) and grease it lightly with oil.
4. Spread 2 tbsp of the batter evenly to make a 100 mm. (4") diameter circle.
5. Cook on both sides till golden brown using ¼ tsp of oil.
6. Remove the *dosa* on a plate, place a portion of the stuffing at an edge and fold it to make a semi-circle.
7. Repeat with the remaining *dosa* batter and stuffing to make 7 more stuffed *dosas*.
Serve hot.

Nutritive values per *dosa*	
Energy	: 110 calories
Protein	: 6.6 gm
Carbohydrates	: 18.1 gm
Fat	: 1.3 gm
Iron	: 1.0 mg
Fibre	: 0.7 mg

Semiyan Upma

Preparation Time: 10 minutes. **Cooking Time:** 12 to 15 minutes. **Serves 4.**

An ideal breakfast that assists weight loss, the fibre rich whole wheat semiyan helps in throwing out excess fats from the body. Moreover, very little coconut and ghee ensures that the calorie count is far less than its original counterpart.

2 cups wheat vermicelli (*semiyan*)
Salt to taste
2 tsp *ghee*
1 tsp mustard seeds (*rai/sarson*)
2 tsp *urad dal* (split black lentils)
6 to 7 curry leaves (*kadi patta*)
⅓ cup finely chopped onions
1 tsp finely chopped green chillies
2 tbsp freshly grated coconut
2 tbsp finely chopped coriander (*dhania*)
Juice of ½ lemon

1. Combine the vermicelli, 2 cups of hot water and little salt in a deep non-stick pan, cover and keep aside for about 5 minutes or till the vermicelli is soft. Drain and keep aside.
2. Heat the ghee in a non-stick *kadhai*, add the mustard seeds and *urad dal* and sauté for a few seconds.
3. When the seeds crackle, add the curry leaves, onions and green chillies and sauté on a medium flame till the onions turn translucent.
4. Add the vermicelli, coconut, coriander, lemon juice and salt, mix well and cook on a medium flame for 2 minutes, while stirring gently. Serve immediately.

Nutritive values per *serving*

Energy	: 115 calories
Protein	: 2.0 gm
Carbohydrates	: 15.7 gm
Fat	: 3.6 gm
Fibre	**: 0.8 gm**

Banana Apple Porridge

Preparation Time: 5 minutes.   Cooking Time: 15 minutes.   Serves 4.

This easy-to-make, simple porridge prepared from broken wheat, oats and fruits, is rich in fibre, calcium and B-complex vitamins – ideal to keep the metabolism going and lose pregnancy weight. I've used low-fat butter and milk to keep the calories down.

¼ cup broken wheat (*dalia*)
2 tsp low-fat butter
2 tbsp quick cooking rolled oats
1½ cups low-fat milk (99.7% fat-free, readily available in the market)
1½ tbsp powdered sugar
½ tsp cinnamon (*dalchini*) powder
1 cup chopped apple
1 cup sliced banana

For the garnish
Apple slices
Banana slices
Cinnamon (*dalchini*) sticks (optional)

1. Clean, wash and drain the broken wheat.
2. Heat the butter in a pressure cooker, add the broken wheat and sauté on a medium flame for 3 to 4 minutes.
3. Add the oats, mix well and sauté on a medium flame for another 2 minutes.
4. Add the milk and 1 cup of water, mix well and pressure cook on a medium flame for 2 whistles.
5. Allow the steam to escape before opening the lid.
6. Add the sugar and cinnamon powder and mix well. Refrigerate to chill.
7. Add the apple and banana and mix well. Serve immediately garnished with apple slices, banana slices and cinnamon sticks.

Nutritive values per serving	
Energy	: 51 calories
Protein	: 3.6 gm
Carbohydrates	: 30.7 gm
Fat	: 1.5 gm
Iron	: 0.8 mg
Calcium	: 88.3 mg
Fibre	: 0.6 gm

Cottage Cheese and Dill Canapés

Preparation Time: 10 minutes. Cooking Time: Nil. Makes 16 canapés.

One of my favorite weight loss snacks, each canapé has only 57 calories. Rich in calcium, it also provides essential fatty acids from olives, which help get the glow back on your skin.

To be mixed into a spread
¾ cup grated low-fat *paneer* (cottage cheese), page 95
2 tbsp thick low-fat curds (*dahi*), page 94
1½ tbsp blanched and finely chopped celery stalks
¼ tsp finely chopped green chillies
6 black olives, cut into thin slices
Salt to taste

Other ingredients
4 whole wheat bread slices
2 tsp low-fat butter

For the garnish
A sprig of coriander (*dhania*)
4 stuffed green olives, cut into slices

1. Divide the spread into 4 equal portions and keep aside.
2. Trim the edges of the bread slices, apply ½ tsp of butter on both sides of each slice and cook them on a non-stick *tava* (griddle) till both the sides are lightly brown in colour.
3. Spread a portion of the spread on one side of each bread slice and cut it into 4 squares. Serve immediately garnished with coriander and stuffed olive slices.

Handy tip:
You may alternatively toast the bread slices in a toaster and then butter them.

Nutritive values per canapé	
Energy	: 57 calories
Protein	: 4.1 gm
Carbohydrates	: 8.4 gm
Fat	: 0.7 gm
Calcium	: 155.3 mg

Soya Poha

Preparation Time: 10 minutes.   Cooking Time: 10 minutes.   Serves 4.
Soaking Time: 15 minutes.

An appetizing alternative to the traditional version, soya poha is rich in protein, iron and zinc. Peas make an appetizing addition to this ideal breakfast when you want to lose weight the healthy way!

1 cup soya granules
2 tsp oil
1 tsp mustard seeds (*rai / sarson*)
8 to 10 curry leaves (*kadi patta*)
¼ tsp asafoetida (*hing*)
½ cup sliced onions
½ tsp finely chopped green chillies
¼ tsp turmeric powder (*haldi*)
2 tbsp boiled green peas
1 tbsp boiled peanuts
1 tbsp lemon juice
Salt to taste

For the garnish
2 tbsp chopped coriander (*dhania*)

1. Soak the soya granules in 2 cups of warm water for 15 minutes. Squeeze thoroughly and keep aside.
2. Heat the oil in a non-stick *kadhai* and add the mustard seeds.
3. When the seeds crackle, add the curry leaves and asafoetida and sauté on a medium flame for a few seconds.
4. Add the onions and green chillies and sauté on a medium flame for another 3 to 4 minutes or till the onions turn translucent.
5. Add the turmeric powder, green peas, peanuts, soya granules, lemon juice and salt, toss gently and cook on a medium flame for 2 to 3 minutes, stirring once in between.
Serve hot garnished with coriander.

Nutritive values per serving

Energy	: 124 calories
Protein	**: 8.9 gm**
Carbohydrates	: 5.9 gm
Fat	: 7.2 gm
Iron	**: 2.1 mg**
Zinc	**: 0.8 mg**
Fibre	**: 0.9 gm**

Muesli

Preparation Time: 5 minutes.   Cooking Time: 5 to 7 minutes.   Serves 4.

Easily put together ingredients in this powerhouse muesli make for a low-cal filling breakfast. Packed with nutrients and fibre, this filling breakfast will surely keep you away from bingeing on unnecessary calorie-laden food.

1 cup quick cooking rolled oats
4 tbsp wheat bran (*konda*)
½ cup cornflakes
¼ tsp vanilla essence
1 tbsp sultanas (*kismis*)

For serving
3 cups warm/ chilled low-fat milk (99.7% fat-free, readily available in the market)
1 cup chopped mixed fruits (apples, orange, strawberries etc.)

1. Combine the oats and wheat bran in a non-stick pan and dry roast on a slow flame for 5 to 7 minutes. Remove and keep aside to cool.
2. Add the cornflakes, vanilla essence and sultanas and toss well.
3. For serving, place ¼ portion of the muesli into a bowl, pour ¾ cup of milk and add ¼ cup of mixed fruits to it and mix well.
4. Repeat with the remaining ingredient to make 3 more servings.
    Serve immediately.

Handy tip: Make the muesli in bulk, use as required and store the remaining in an air-tight container.

Nutritive values per serving
Energy	: 201 calories
Protein	: 10.2 gm
Carbohydrates	: 35.0 gm
Fat	: 2.2 gm
Iron	**: 3.1 mg**
Zinc	**: 1.2 mg**
Calcium	**: 258.7 mg**
Fibre	**: 2.1 gm**

Soups and Salads

Garlic Vegetable Soup

Preparation Time: 10 minutes. Cooking Time: 15 minutes. Serves 4.

A delicious soup to begin your meals with or to be had as a mid-morning snack. I've flavoured it with garlic and added loads of mixed veggies to create a colourful and nourishing fare. Low-fat milk keeps the calorie content of this soup low.

2 tsp oil
¼ cup finely chopped onions
2 tsp finely chopped garlic (*lehsun*)
1 cup finely chopped mixed vegetables (baby corn, broccoli, carrots, asparagus etc.)
1½ cups hot low-fat milk (99.7% fat-free, readily available in the market)
Salt and freshly ground pepper to taste
2 tbsp quick cooking rolled oats

1. Heat the oil in a deep non-stick pan, add the onions and garlic and sauté on a medium flame for 2 minutes.
2. Add the mixed vegetables and sauté on a medium flame for another 2 minutes.
3. Add the milk, 1½ cups of hot water, salt and pepper, mix well and bring to boil.
4. Add the oats, mix well and simmer for 5 minutes or till the soup thickens.
   Serve hot.

Nutritive values per serving

Energy	: 75 calories
Protein	: 3.6 gm
Carbohydrates	: 9.1 gm
Fat	: 2.9 gm
Folic acid	: 10.5 mcg
Calcium	: 124.7 mg
Fibre	: 0.5 gm

Nourishing Moong Soup

Preparation Time: 5 minutes.   Cooking Time: 20 minutes.   Serves 4.

Subtly flavoured with curry leaves and lemon juice, this moong soup is easily digestible and high on energy. Carrots and paneer increase the protein and vitamin A content making this soup a great starter to meals.

½ cup *moong* (*whole green gram*)
1 tsp oil
¼ tsp cumin seeds (*jeera*)
4 to 5 curry leaves (*kadi patta*)
¼ tsp asafoetida (*hing*)
Salt to taste
2 tsp lemon juice

For the garnish
2 tbsp finely chopped coriander (*dhania*)

1. Clean and wash the *moong*, add 5 cups of water and pressure cook for 3 to 4 whistles.
2. Allow the steam to escape before opening the lid.
3. Heat the oil in a deep non-stick pan and add the cumin seeds.
4. When the seeds crackle, add the curry leaves, asafoetida, cooked *moong* (along with the water) and salt, mix well and bring to boil.
5. Add the lemon juice and mix well.
Serve hot garnished with coriander.

Handy tip:
To enhance the nutritive value of the soup, add ¼ cup of low-fat chopped *paneer* and ¼ cup of grated carrots after step 4 and simmer till the carrots are tender.

Nutritive values per serving	
Energy	: 80 calories
Protein	**: 4.9 gm**
Carbohydrates	: 11.6 gm
Fat	: 1.5 gm
Calcium	**: 27.9 mg**

Carrot and Coriander Soup

Preparation Time: 8 to 10 minutes.   **Cooking Time:** 15 to 20 minutes.   **Serves 4.**

Ample carrots and coriander in this yummy soup fulfill up to ¾th of your daily vitamin A requirement. While keeping the calorie count down to only 36 calories, this soup wins the ultimate soup for weight-watchers award!

1 tsp oil
1 cup finely sliced onions
2 cups carrot cubes
1 cup finely chopped coriander (*dhania*)
Salt and freshly ground pepper to taste

For the garnish
A few carrot strips

1. Heat the oil in a pressure cooker, add the onions and sauté on a medium flame for 2 minutes.
2. Add the carrots and ½ cup of coriander and sauté on a medium flame for another 3 to 4 minutes.
3. Add 4 cups of hot water and salt, mix well and and pressure cook on a high flame for 2 whistles.
4. Allow the steam to escape before opening the lid.
5. When slightly cool, blend in a mixer till smooth.
6. Transfer the mixture to a deep non-stick pan and bring to boil.
7. Add the pepper and remaining ½ cup of coriander and mix well.
   Serve immediately garnished with carrot strips.

Nutritive values per serving	
Energy	: 36 calories
Protein	: 0.6 gm
Carbohydrates	: 5.2 gm
Fat	: 1.4 gm
Vitamin A	**: 996.5 mcg**
Calcium	**: 41.9 mg**

Green Pea Soup

Preparation Time: 10 minutes.   Cooking Time: 15 to 20 minutes.   Serves 4.

This amazing protein rich soup is a unique combination of peas and onions. Flavoured with garlic, I love this low-cal version of creamy soup for its simplicity and texture.

1 tsp oil
1¼ cups chopped onions
2 tsp finely chopped garlic (*lehsun*)
1½ cups fresh green peas
Salt and freshly ground pepper to taste

1. Heat the oil in a deep non-stick pan, add the onions and garlic and sauté on a medium flame till the onions turn translucent.
2. Add the green peas, salt and 4 cups of hot water, mix well and simmer for 12 to 15 minutes or till the peas are cooked.
3. When slightly cool, blend in a mixer till smooth.
4. Transfer the mixture to a deep non-stick pan, add the pepper and bring to boil.
   Serve hot.

Nutritive values per serving

Energy	: 81 calories
Protein	: 4.3 gm
Carbohydrates	: 13.0 gm
Fat	: 1.3 gm
Calcium	: 31.8 mg
Iron	: 1.2 mg
Fibre	: 2.4 gm

Hot Borscht

Preparation Time: 10 minutes.   Cooking Time: 10 to 12 minutes.   Serves 4.

Beetroot, ample veggies and low-fat hung curds make for a delicious, filling soup. Combine this special soup from Russia with multi-grain bread to make a great evening snack that's mild in taste and high in folic acid to prevent anaemia.

1 tsp olive oil
⅓ cup thinly sliced onions
¾ cup grated beetroot
½ cup thinly sliced potatoes
½ cup thickly grated carrots
¾ cup shredded cabbage
½ cup thinly sliced tomatoes
Salt and freshly ground pepper to taste

For the garnish
2 tbsp low-fat hung curds (*dahi*), page 94
4 tsp finely chopped celery (*ajmoda*)

1. Heat the oil in a deep non-stick pan, add the onions and sauté on a medium flame for a minute.
2. Add the beetroot, potatoes, carrots, cabbage and tomatoes, mix well and sauté on a medium flame for another 2 minutes.
3. Add 3 cups of hot water, mix well and simmer for 5 to 7 minutes.
4. Place equal quantities of soup in 4 individual bowls and garnish each bowl with ½ tbsp of curds and 1 tsp of celery.
   Serve immediately.

Nutritive values per serving

Energy	: 43 calories
Protein	: 1.2 gm
Carbohydrates	: 6.6 gm
Fat	: 1.4 gm
Vitamin C	**: 27.0 mg**
Folic acid	**: 11.4 mcg**

Spicy Stir-Fry Soup

Preparation Time: 10 to 12 minutes.   Cooking Time: 10 minutes.   Serves 4.
Soaking Time: 15 minutes.

A visual delight, this clear soup has stir-fried sprouts and veggies to up the protein, vitamin C and iron content. Ready in minutes and spiced with garlic and chillies, it is an ideal way to satiate hunger pangs without gorging on too much food.

3 whole dry Kashmiri red chillies, deseeded
4 cloves garlic (*lehsun*)
2 tsp low-fat butter
2 spring onions, sliced
½ cup shredded cabbage
1 red capsicum, cut into thin strips
¼ cup bean sprouts
2 tsp lemon juice
¼ tsp sugar
Salt to taste

1. Put 2 cups of water to boil.
2. Soak the red chillies in ½ cup of hot water for 15 minutes (Keep the remaining 1½ cups of water aside for later use).
3. Drain, combine with the garlic and pound using a mortar-pestle (*khalbhatta*) to a smooth paste. Keep aside.
4. Heat the butter in a deep non-stick pan, add the chilli-garlic paste and sauté on a medium flame for a few seconds.
5. Add the spring onions, cabbage, capsicum and bean sprouts and sauté on a medium flame for another few seconds.
6. Add the remaining 1½ cups of hot water, lemon juice, sugar and salt, mix well and bring to boil. Serve hot.

Nutritive values per serving

Energy	: 54 calories
Protein	: 3.0 gm
Carbohydrates	: 8.2 gm
Fat	: 1.2 gm
Vitamin C	: 68.8 mg
Iron	: 1.0 mg
Fibre	: 1.3 gm

Dalia and Vegetable Salad

Preparation Time: 10 minutes.   Cooking Time: 7 to 8 minutes.   Serves 4.

Here's a nutrient-rich, delicious treat with assorted vegetables and dalia with a delicately flavoured mint dressing. The best part is, it has just 48 calories per serving – a surefire way to lose weight!

To be mixed into a dressing
¼ cup finely chopped mint leaves (*phudina*)
1 tbsp lemon juice
Salt and freshly ground pepper to taste

Other ingredients
½ tsp oil
Salt to taste
½ cup cooked broken wheat (*dalia*)
1 cup cucumber cubes
½ cup chopped tomatoes
½ cup broccoli florets
½ cup sliced mushrooms (*khumbh*)
1 cup lettuce, torn into pieces

1. Boil a vesselful of water, add the oil and salt and mix well.
2. Add the broken wheat and boil for 6 to 7 minutes.
3. Drain, wash with cold water and drain again.
4. Add all the remaining ingredients in a bowl, pour the dressing over it and toss well.
5. Keep refrigerated for at least 1 hour. Serve chilled.

Nutritive values per serving	
Energy	: 48 calories
Protein	: 2.4 gm
Carbohydrates	: 8.4 gm
Fat	: 0.7 gm
Vitamin C	**: 26.0 mg**
Folic acid	**: 23.5 mcg**
Fibre	**: 1.0 gm**

Sprouts and Vegetable Salad

Preparation Time: 10 minutes.   Cooking time: Nil.   Serves 4.

Keep yourself satiated with this salad that is a winning combination of sprouts and veggies. Sprouts are rich in iron, fibre, vitamin C and vitamin B-complex, making this a great weight-loss salad. I've kept the preparation simple by adding coriander, lemon juice and pepper.

1 cup boiled mixed sprouts (*kala chana, chawli, moong, rajma* etc.)
½ cup chopped cucumber
¼ cup chopped purple cabbage
¼ cup grated carrots
2 tbsp chopped tomatoes
¼ tsp freshly ground pepper
1 tbsp lemon juice
1 tsp sugar
2 tbsp finely chopped coriander (*dhania*)
Salt to taste

Combine all the ingredients in a serving bowl and toss well. Keep aside for 15 minutes so that the flavours blend well.
 Serve immediately.

Nutritive values per serving	
Energy	: 76 calories.
Protein	: 4.0 gm
Carbohydrates	: 13.5 gm
Fat	: 0.6 gm
Vitamin C	**: 12.8 mg**
Folic Acid	**: 18.6 mcg**
Iron	**: 1.1 mg**
Fibre	**: 1.0 gm**

Summer Salad

Preparation Time: 15 minutes.   Cooking Time: Nil.   Serves 4.

Low in calories but high in fibre, here's a salad with an unusual flavoursome dressing made of lemon, honey and ginger. Watermelon, pineapple, cucumber, papaya and sweet corn together make this a colourful dish. Vitamin A and C act as antioxidants and help in collagen synthesis, which assists post-pregnancy skin renewal and tightening.

To be mixed together into ginger dressing
½ tsp grated ginger (*adrak*)
2 tsp lemon juice
1 tsp honey
1 tbsp fresh low-fat curds (*dahi*), page 94
1 tbsp skim milk powder
Salt to taste

Other ingredients
1 cup watermelon cubes
1 cup pineapple cubes
1 cup sliced cucumber
¾ cup papaya cubes
2 tbsp cooked sweet corn kernels (*makai ke dane*)
Salt to taste

For the garnish
2 tbsp grated carrots

1. Refrigerate the dressing to chill.
2. Combine the watermelon, pineapple, cucumber, papaya, corn and salt in a bowl and toss well. Refrigerate to chill.
3. Just before serving, pour the chilled ginger dressing over the salad and toss gently. Serve immediately garnished with carrots.

Nutritive values per serving	
Energy	: 67 calories
Protein	: 2.3 gm
Carbohydrates	: 14.2 gm
Fat	: 0.3 gm
Fibre	**: 0.9 gm**
Iron	**: 4.6 mg**
Vitamin C	**: 36.3 mg**

Citrus Salad

Preparation Time: 20 minutes. Cooking time: Nil. Serves 4.

Macaroni, veggies, sprouts and fruits in a refreshing mint flavoured curd dressing create a wholesome salad. Keep hunger pangs at bay and get back to shape!

To be mixed into a mint dressing
¾ cup thick fresh low-fat curds (*dahi*), page 94
3 tbsp finely chopped mint leaves (*phudina*)
¾ tsp mustard (*rai/ sarson*) powder
¾ tsp powdered sugar
Salt to taste

Other ingredients
¼ cup cooked whole wheat pasta, refer handy tip
½ cup chopped coloured capsicum (red, yellow and green)
½ cup chopped carrots, blanched
1 spring onion white, chopped
2 tbsp finely chopped spring onion greens
1 cup bean sprouts
½ cup orange segments
½ cup sweet lime segments

1. Combine all the ingredients in a bowl and refrigerate to chill.
2. Just before serving, add the chilled dressing and toss well.
   Serve immediately.

Handy tip :
Whole wheat pasta is nutrient and fibre rich. Vegetables and fruits added along with it balances the nutrient quotient of this salad.

Nutritive values per serving

Energy	: 97 calories
Protein	: 5.7 gm
Carbohydrates	: 17.9 gm
Fat	: 0.5 gm
Vitamin C	**: 45.6 mg**
Fibre	**: 1.4 gm**

Fruity Sprouts Salad

Preparation Time: 15 minutes.   Cooking Time: Nil.   Serves 4.

Here's a fruity sprouts salad rich in beneficial ingredients – papaya aids digestion, curds boost the immune system and improve skin texture. Very satiating, specially when you are on diet and restrict your food intake. It's all in the dressing is all I can say about this crunchy and sweet salad!

To be blended into fruity dressing
½ cup papaya cubes
¼ cup low-fat thick curds (*dahi*), page 94
1 tbsp powdered sugar

Other ingredients
½ cup boiled mixed sprouts (*kala chana, chawli, moong, rajma* etc.)
½ cup apple cubes, with the skin
½ cup pomegranate (*anardana*)
½ cup roughly chopped spinach (*palak*)
Salt to taste

1. Combine all the ingredients in a bowl and refrigerate to chill.
2. Just before serving, add the chilled dressing and toss well.
   Serve immediately.

Nutritive values per serving	
Energy	: 47 calories
Protein	: 2.0 gm
Carbohydrates	: 9.1 gm
Fat	: 0.2 gm
Fibre	**: 0.9 gm**
Vitamin C	**: 16.0 mg**
Vitamin A	**: 634.2 mcg**

Snacks

Stuffed Spinach Pancakes

Preparation Time: 10 minutes.   Cooking Time: 10 minutes.   Makes 4 stuffed pancakes.

Yummy…is all you will say as you enjoy this low-calorie, wholesome pancake stuffed with spinach and mozzarella cheese. An ideal snack for evenings!

For the batter
¼ cup whole wheat flour (*gehun ka atta*)
¼ cup *maida* (plain flour)
¼ cup low-fat milk (99.7% fat-free, readily available in the market)
Salt to taste

For the stuffing
1 tsp low-fat butter
¼ cup chopped onions
1 tsp finely chopped garlic (*lehsun*)
½ cup chopped tomatoes
¾ cup chopped spinach (*palak*)
2 tbsp grated mozzarella cheese
Salt to taste

Other ingredients
1 tsp oil for cooking

For the batter
Combine all the ingredients in a bowl along with ½ cup of water and mix well to make a smooth batter. Keep aside.

For the stuffing
1. Heat butter in a non-stick pan, add the onions and garlic and sauté on a medium flame for 2 minutes.
2. Add the tomatoes and sauté on a medium flame for another 3 to 4 minutes.
3. Add the spinach and sauté on a high flame for 2 to 3 minutes.
4. Remove from the flame, add the cheese and mix well. Keep aside.

How to proceed
1. Heat a non-stick pan, pour a ladleful of the batter and tilt the pan around quickly so that the batter coats the pan evenly.
2. Cook the pancake on both the sides using ¼ tsp of oil for 30 seconds approximately.
3. Remove the pancake on a plate and spread ¼ᵗʰ of the stuffing on one half of the pancake.
4. Fold the pancake over the stuffing to make a semi-circle and press it lightly.
5. Repeat with the remaining ingredients to make 3 more stuffed pancakes.
Serve immediately.

Nutritive values per pancake
Energy	: 89 calories
Protein	: 3.4 gm
Carbohydrate	: 12.4 gm
Fat	: 2.8 gm
Fibre	: 0.4 mg
Vitamin A	: 890.2 mcg
Calcium	: 69.3 mg
Folic acid	: 24.3 mcg

Variation:

You can be innovative by using different stuffings for the pancake. Try the cauliflower stuffing given below as a variation and relish a new snack.

For the cauliflower stuffing
1 tsp oil
1 tsp finely chopped green chillies
½ tsp grated ginger (*adrak*)
¼ cup finely chopped onions
¾ cup grated cauliflower
¼ cup grated low-fat *paneer* (cottage cheese), page 95
¼ tsp turmeric powder (*haldi*)
Salt to taste
2 tbsp finely chopped coriander (*dhania*)

For the cauliflower stuffing
1. Heat the oil in a small non-stick *kadhai*, add the green chillies, ginger and onions and sauté on a medium flame for 2 to 3 minutes.
2. Add the cauliflower, sprinkle a little water and sauté on a slow flame for 3 to 4 minutes or till the cauliflower is cooked.
3. Add the *paneer*, turmeric powder, salt and coriander, mix well and cook on a slow flame for 2 minutes, while stirring gently. Use as per the recipe.

Masala Chana

Preparation Time: 20 minutes. Cooking Time: 10 minutes. Serves 4.
Soaking Time: Overnight.

Boiled chana, tomato and onion salad, with just the right dash of lemon juice, green chillies and kairi – a nutritious and tasty snack that provides complex carbohydrates. A great way to lose weight while maintaining post-delivery health.

2 tsp low-fat butter
2 tsp finely chopped green chillies
½ cup finely chopped onions
¾ cup finely chopped tomatoes
½ tsp chilli powder (optional)
¼ tsp *garam masala*
1 tbsp *chaat masala*
½ cup boiled, peeled and finely chopped potatoes
1 cup *kala chana* (brown chick peas) / *hara chana* (green chick peas), soaked overnight and cooked
Salt to taste
1½ tbsp finely chopped raw mangoes (*kairi*)
1 tbsp finely chopped coriander (*dhania*)
1 tbsp lemon juice

1. Heat the butter in a non-stick *kadhai*, add the green chillies and onions and sauté on a medium flame for 3 to 4 minutes or till the onions turn translucent.
2. Add the tomatoes, chilli powder, *garam masala* and *chaat masala* and sauté on a medium flame for 2 to 3 minutes.
3. Add the potatoes, *chana*, salt, raw mangoes, coriander and lemon juice, mix well and sauté on a medium flame for another 2 to 3 minutes. Serve immediately.

Nutritive values per serving	
Energy	: 78 calories
Protein	: 4.0 gm
Carbohydrate	: 12.0 gm
Fat	: 1.4 gm
Vitamin A	**: 438.0 mcg**
Fibre	**: 2.0 gm**

Dry Figs and Banana Smoothie

Preparation Time: 5 minutes.   Cooking Time: Nil.   Makes 4 glasses.
Soaking time: ½ hour.

A filling mid-morning snack, this smoothie uses naturally sweet dried figs. With the use of low-fat curds, milk and minimum amount of sugar, the calorie content has been reduced substantially.

3 cups chilled low-fat milk (99.7% fat-free, readily available in the market)
1 cup sliced banana
4 tsp sugar
8 dried figs (*anjeer*), soaked for ½ hour and chopped
8 tbsp fresh low-fat curds (*dahi*), page 94

For the garnish
2 cashewnuts (*kaju*), cut into halves

1. Combine all the ingredients and blend in a mixer till smooth.
2. Pour equal quantities of the smoothie in 4 individual glasses and garnish each glass with a cashewnut half.
   Serve immediately.

Nutritive values per glass	
Energy	: 154 calories
Protein	: 7.3 gm
Carbohydrates	: 19.5 gm
Fat	: 3.4 gm
Vitamin A	: 447.2 mcg
Calcium	: 303.4 mg
Fibre	: 0.8 gm

Mini Sprouts Uttapa

Preparation Time: 10 minutes. Cooking Time: 20 minutes.
Serves 4 (Makes approx. 8 mini *uttapas*).

The nursing mother will find this quick and easy snack both nutritious and delicious. Using sprouted pulses substantially increases the iron, calcium and protein content. With very little oil, the uttapas make a great low-cal evening snack.

To be mixed together into a batter
½ cup rice flour (*chawal ka atta*)
¼ cup peeled and grated potatoes
1 tbsp roasted peanuts, crushed
¼ cup water
Salt to taste

To be mixed together for the topping
½ cup boiled mixed sprouts (*kala chana, chawli, moong, rajma* etc.), roughly chopped
2 tbsp finely chopped coriander (*dhania*)
1 green chilli, finely chopped
Salt to taste

Other ingredients
1¼ tsp oil for greasing and cooking

1. Divide the topping into 8 equal portions. Keep aside.
2. Heat a non-stick *tava* (griddle), lightly grease it using ¼ tsp of oil and spread 1½ tbsp of the batter to make a 75 mm. (3") diameter circle.
3. Spread a portion of the topping evenly over it.
4. Cook using ⅛ tsp of oil till both sides are golden brown in colour.
5. Repeat with the remaining ingredients to make 7 more *uttapas*.
Serve hot.

Nutritive values per serving	
Energy	: 100 calories
Protein	: 3.0 gm
Carbohydrates	: 16.1 gm
Fat	: 2.6 gm
Calcium	: 14.2 mg
Iron	: 0.5 mg
Fibre	: 0.5 gm

Poha and Oats Chivda

Preparation Time: 10 minutes. **Cooking Time:** 5 to 7 minutes. **Serves 4.**

Fibre rich oats, iron rich poha and protein rich chana dal make for a healthy variation of the traditional fried chivda. Make in bulk and store it in an air-tight container. Enjoy it as a snack without worrying about straying from your weight-loss regime.

2 tsp oil
¼ tsp mustard seeds (*rai / sarson*)
2 green chillies, slit lengthwise
6 to 8 curry leaves (*kadi patta*)
A pinch asafoetida (*hing*)
A pinch turmeric powder (*haldi*)
1 cup quick cooking rolled oats, roasted
½ cup poha (rice flakes), roasted
1 *urad dal papad*, roasted and crushed
¼ cup roasted *chana dal* (*daria dal*)
1 tsp powdered sugar
Salt to taste

1. Heat the oil in a non-stick pan, add the mustard seeds, green chillies and curry leaves.
2. When the seeds crackle, add the asafoetida and turmeric powder and mix well.
3. Add the oats, *poha*, *papad*, *chana dal*, sugar and salt and toss well. Cool and store in an air-tight container.

Nutritive values per serving	
Energy	: 147 calories
Protein	: **5.7 gm**
Carbohydrates	: 25.6 gm
Fat	: 3.6 gm
Iron	: **2.7 mg**
Fibre	: 1.3 gm

Hariyali Chanki

Preparation Time: 10 to 12 minutes.   Cooking Time: 15 minutes.
Serves 4 (makes approx. 30 *chankis*).

Green as its name suggests, this non-fried snack combines seven green veggies with four different flours. Rich in iron, folic acid and fibre, it assists in hemoglobin production. A great alternative to oil laden snacks – ideal for health conscious mothers who want to lose weight the healthy way.

¼ cup whole wheat flour (*gehun ka atta*)
1 tbsp *besan* (Bengal gram flour)
1 tbsp *ragi* /*nachni* (red millet) flour
1 tbsp soya flour
1½ tbsp finely chopped mint leaves (*phudina*)
1½ tbsp finely chopped spinach (*palak*)
1½ tbsp finely chopped fresh basil leaves
1½ tbsp finely chopped coriander (*dhania*)
1½ tbsp finely chopped dill leaves (*shepu* / *suva bhaji*)
1½ tbsp finely chopped fenugreek leaves (*methi*)
1½ tbsp finely chopped radish leaves (*mooli ke patte*)
1 tbsp sesame seeds (*til*)
1 tsp ginger-green chilli paste
¼ tsp turmeric powder (*haldi*)
1½ tbsp low-fat curds (*dahi*), page 94
Salt to taste
2¼ tsp oil for kneading and cooking
Whole wheat flour (*gehun ka atta*) for rolling

1. Combine all the ingredients in a bowl and knead into a soft dough using enough water. Keep aside for 5 minutes.
2. Knead again using ¼ tsp of oil till smooth and divide the dough into 30 equal portions.
3. Sprinkle a little flour on a clean dry surface, place a portion of the dough and pat it lightly using your fingers to make a thick 25 mm. (1") diameter *chanki*.
4. Cook the *chanki* on a non-stick *tava* (griddle), using a little oil till both sides are golden brown in colour.
Serve immediately.

Handy tip: Roll a few *chankis* at a time and cook them in batches on the *tava*.

Nutritive values per serving	
Energy	: 93 calories
Protein	: 3.6 gm
Carbohydrates	: 9.7 gm
Fat	: 4.8 gm
Iron	**: 2.0 mg**
Folic acid	**: 16.0 mcg**
Fibre	**: 0.5 gm**

Soya Sesame Khakhra

Preparation Time: 10 minutes. Cooking Time: 20 minutes. Makes 6 *khakhras*.

Made from soya flour and calcium and iron rich sesame seeds, these khakhras make a perfect anytime snack. Light on calories, wholesome in nutrition; store them in an air-tight container, to keep them crisp and fresh.

½ cup soya flour
¼ cup whole wheat flour (*gehun ka atta*)
4 tsp sesame seeds (*til*), black and white
Salt to taste
¼ tsp oil for kneading
Whole wheat flour (*gehun ka atta*) for rolling
1½ tsp ghee for cooking

1. Combine the soya flour, wheat flour, sesame seeds and salt in a bowl and knead to form a soft dough using enough warm water. Cover with a wet muslin cloth and keep aside.
2. Knead again using oil till smooth and divide the dough into 6 equal portions.
3. Roll out each portion into a 125 mm. (5") diameter thin circle, using a little wheat flour for rolling.
4. Heat a non-stick *tava* (griddle) and cook each *khakhra* on a slow flame using ¼ tsp ghee till pink spots appear on both the sides.
5. Continue cooking the *khakhra* on a slow flame while pressing with a folded muslin cloth till it turns brown and crisp.
   Serve immediately or store in an air-tight container.

Nutritive values per *khakhra*	
Energy	: 60 calories
Protein	**: 4.4 gm**
Carbohydrates	: 4.7 gm
Fat	: 2.7 gm
Calcium	**: 15.8 mg**
Iron	**: 0.8 mg**

Pineapple Stir-Fry

Preparation Time: 15 minutes. Cooking Time: 6 to 8 minutes. Serves 4.

Revive your taste buds with aromatic pineapple and exotic veggies stir-fried in soya sauce. Spicy and tangy, here's a nourishing snack, which also keeps the metabolism high.

2 tsp oil
1 tsp dry red chilli flakes
½ cup pineapple cubes
½ cup carrot cubes, blanched
½ cup zucchini cubes, blanched
½ cup bean sprouts
½ cup baby corn, cut into 25 mm. (1") pieces and blanched
½ cup shredded cabbage
½ red capsicum, cut into cubes
½ cup thinly sliced spring onion whites
Salt to taste
½ cup finely chopped spring onion greens
½ cup fresh pineapple juice
2 tsp soya sauce
1 tsp sugar

1. Heat the oil in a wok on a high flame, add the chilli flakes, pineapple, carrots, zucchini, bean sprouts, baby corn, cabbage, capsicum, spring onion whites and salt and stir-fry on a high flame for 3 to 4 minutes.
2. Add the spring onion greens, pineapple juice, soya sauce and sugar and stir-fry on a high flame for another 3 to 4 minutes. Serve immediately.

Nutritive values per serving

Energy	: 133 calories
Protein	: 5.5 gm
Carbohydrates	: 22.1 gm
Fat	: 2.9 gm
Vitamin C	: 74.8 mg
Iron	: 2.5 mg
Fibre	: 2.1 gm

Baby Corn Paneer Jalfrazie

Preparation Time: 10 minutes.   Cooking Time: 10 minutes.   Serves 4.

New mothers will relish this exotic riot of colours with spring onion, baby corn and capsicum. This recipe certainly gets my vote for being balanced with ample protein, vitamins and minerals from the low-fat paneer and veggies.

2 tsp oil
½ cup sliced spring onions whites
1¼ cups sliced coloured capsicum (red, yellow and green)
12 baby corn, cut into 4 lengthwise
¼ tsp turmeric powder (*haldi*)
½ tsp chilli powder
½ tsp coriander-cumin seeds (*dhania-jeera*) powder
¾ cup sliced tomatoes
2 tbsp tomato ketchup
2 tbsp tomato purée
¼ cup chopped low-fat *paneer* (cottage cheese), page 95
½ cup chopped spring onion greens
1 tsp vinegar
½ tsp *garam masala*
¼ tsp sugar
Salt to taste

1. Heat the oil in a non-stick *kadhai*, add the spring onion whites, coloured capsicum and sauté on a medium flame till the onions turn golden brown in colour.
2. Add the baby corn, turmeric powder, chilli powder, coriander-cumin seeds powder, tomatoes, tomato ketchup and tomato purée and sauté on a slow flame for 4 to 5 minutes or till the baby corn is cooked.
3. Add the *paneer*, spring onion greens, vinegar, *garam masala*, sugar and salt, toss gently and cook on a medium flame for another minute. Serve hot.

Nutritive values per serving

Energy	: 165 calories
Protein	**: 6.6 gm**
Carbohydrates	: 28.9 gm
Fat	: 3.4 gm
Iron	**: 1.1 mg**
Vitamin C	**: 71.6 mg**
Calcium	**: 219.9 mg**
Fibre	**: 1.9 gm**

Rice and Dal

Tendli Bhaat

Preparation Time: 10 minutes. Cooking Time: 20 minutes. Serves 4.
Soaking time: 10 minutes.

Nutritious tendli comes together with spicy rice for a delicious change from the usual rice and dal. I have reduced the quantity of coconut to retain its original flavour while keeping the dish low-cal. Serve it with low-fat curds to mellow the spices and make up a wholesome meal.

To be ground into a spice powder
2 cloves (*laung/ lavang*), roasted
12 mm. (½") piece cinnamon (*dalchini*)
1 tsp coriander seeds (*dhania*), roasted
1 tsp cumin seeds (*jeera*), roasted
1 tsp caraway seeds (*shah jeera*), roasted
2 tbsp grated dry coconut (*kopra*)
1 tbsp sesame seeds (*til*)

Other ingredients
1 cup brown rice / long grained rice (*Basmati*)
2 tsp oil
½ tsp mustard seeds (*rai/ sarson*)
½ tsp cumin seeds (*jeera*)
2 cardamom (*elaichi*)
12 mm. (½") piece cinnamon (*dalchini*)
1 clove (*laung/ lavang*)
¼ tsp fenugreek seeds (*methi*)
2 green chillies, slit
5 curry leaves (*kadi patta*)
¼ tsp asafoetida (*hing*)
1½ cups *tendli*, sliced horizontally
½ tsp turmeric powder (*haldi*)
½ tsp chilli powder
Salt to taste

For the garnish
2 to 3 coconut slices
6 to 7 curry leaves (*kadi patta*)

1. Wash and soak the rice for about 10 minutes. Drain and keep aside.
2. Heat the oil in a non-stick *kadhai* and add the mustard seeds.
3. When the seeds crackle, add the cumin seeds, cardamom, cinnamon, clove, fenugreek seeds, green chillies, curry leaves and asafoetida and sauté on a medium flame for a few seconds.
4. Add the *tendli* and rice and sauté on a medium flame for a few minutes.
5. Add the turmeric powder, chilli powder, half of the spice powder and salt and sauté on a medium flame for a minute.
6. Add 2¼ cups of hot water and simmer till the rice is tender.
7. Add the remaining half of the spice powder, mix gently and cover and simmer for another 2 minutes.

Serve hot garnished with coconut slices and curry leaves.

Nutritive values per serving
Energy	: 215 calories
Protein	: 4.9 gm
Carbohydrates	: 36.5 gm
Fat	: 5.8 gm
Calcium	**: 66.9 mg**
Zinc	**: 1.0 mg**
Fibre	**: 0.8 gm**

Ram Khichdi

Preparation Time: 15 minutes.   Cooking Time: 20 minutes.   Serves 4.
Soaking Time: 10 to 15 minutes.

Shed extra pounds with this easy-to-make khichdi. The perfect combination of dal and rice makes this khichdi protein-rich. Mixed veggies add loads of essential nutrients – fibre, iron, calcium and zinc. Enjoy this spicy one dish meal wonder with low-fat curds.

½ cup uncooked brown rice / rice (*chawal*)
½ cup yellow *moong dal* (split yellow gram)
1 tsp ghee
½ tsp cumin seeds (*jeera*)
2 cloves (*laung / lavang*)
25 mm. (1") stick cinnamon (*dalchini*)
1 bayleaf (*tejpatta*)
½ cup cauliflower florets
½ cup chopped brinjal (*baingan / eggplant*)
½ cup peeled and chopped potatoes
½ cup chopped onions
¼ cup chopped French beans
¼ cup green peas
½ tsp turmeric powder *(haldi)*
1 tsp chilli powder
½ tsp *garam masala*
Salt to taste

1. Clean, wash and soak the rice and *moong dal* in enough water for 10 to 15 minutes. Drain and keep aside.
2. Heat the ghee in a pressure cooker and add the cumin seeds, cloves, cinnamon and bayleaf.
3. When the cumin seeds crackle, add all the vegetables, turmeric powder, chilli powder and *garam masala* and sauté on a medium flame for 3 to 4 minutes.
4. Add the rice and *moong dal*, mix well and sauté on a medium flame for another 2 minutes.
5. Add 4 cups of hot water, mix well and pressure cook for 3 to 4 whistles.
6. Allow the steam to escape before opening the lid and mix gently.
   Serve hot.

Nutritive values per serving

Energy	: 178 calories
Protein	**: 7.5 gm**
Carbohydrates	: 33.2 gm
Fat	: 1.7 gm
Calcium	**: 32.0 mg**
Iron	**: 1.3 mg**
Zinc	**: 1.1 mg**
Fibre	**: 1.1 gm**

Vegetable Pulao

Preparation Time: 10 minutes.   Cooking Time: 20 to 25 minutes.   Serves 4.
Soaking Time: 10 to 15 minutes.

An aromatic pulao with low-cal but vitamin A rich chunky mushroom and mixed vegetables – best served with vegetable raita.

1¼ cups brown rice / long grained rice (*Basmati*)
1 tsp ghee
50 mm. (2") stick cinnamon (*dalchini*)
2 cloves (*laung / lavang*)
2 cardamom (*elaichi*)
2 bayleaves (*tejpatta*)
⅓ cup sliced onions
⅓ cup sliced carrots
⅓ cup sliced French beans
⅓ cup sliced mushrooms (*khumbh*)
⅓ cup fresh green peas
Salt to taste

1. Clean, wash and soak the rice in enough water for atleast 10 to 15 minutes. Drain and keep aside.
2. Heat the ghee in a non-stick *kadhai*, add the cinnamon, cloves, cardamom and bayleave and sauté on a medium flame for a few seconds.
3. Add the onions, carrots, French beans, mushrooms, green peas, rice and salt, mix well and sauté on a medium flame for another minute.
4. Add 3 cups of hot water, mix well and cook on a slow flame for 15 to 20 minutes or till the rice gets cooked and the water has evaporated. Serve hot.

Nutritive values per serving	
Energy	: 178 calories
Protein	: 4.9 gm
Carbohydrates	: 46.1 gm
Fat	: 1.6 gm
Vitamin A	**: 163.8 mcg**
Zinc	**: 0.8 mg**
Fibre	**: 0.9 gm**

Tava Sprouts Pulao

Preparation Time: 20 minutes.   Cooking Time: 15 minutes.   Serves 4.

The famous tava rice has been given a healthy makeover – I've added sprouts which makes it rich in protein, iron, zinc and fibre. Veggies spiced with pav bhaji masala add just the right touch of flavour!

2 tsp oil
2 tsp cumin seeds (*jeera*)
½ cup chopped onions
1 tsp finely chopped ginger (*adrak*)
1 tsp finely chopped garlic (*lehsun*)
1 cup chopped tomatoes
½ cup chopped capsicum
½ tsp chilli powder
A pinch turmeric powder (*haldi*)
1 tsp *pav bhaji masala*
½ cup boiled *moong* (whole green gram) sprouts
½ cup boiled *matki* (moath beans) sprouts
1½ cups cooked brown rice / long grained rice (*Basmati*)
Salt to taste

For the garnish
2 tbsp chopped mint leaves (*phudina*)

1. Heat the oil in a non-stick *kadhai* and add the cumin seeds.
2. When the seeds crackle, add the onions, ginger and garlic and sauté on a medium flame till they turn translucent.
3. Add the tomatoes, ¼ cup of water and cook on a medium flame for 5 minutes.
4. Add the capsicum, chilli powder, turmeric powder and *pav bhaji masala*, mix well and cook on a medium flame for another 2 minutes.
5. Add the *moong* sprouts, *matki* sprouts, rice and salt, toss gently well and cook for 2 to 3 minutes.
   Serve hot garnished with the mint leaves.

Nutritive values per serving	
Energy	: 199 calories
Protein	**: 6.2 gm**
Carbohydrates	: 36.8 gm
Fat	: 3.0 gm
Iron	**: 1.1 mg**
Zinc	**: 0.7 mg**
Fibre	**: 1.2 gm**

Bengali Khichdi

Preparation Time: 15 minutes.   Cooking Time: 30 to 35 minutes.   Serves 4.
Soaking Time: 15 minutes

You will love this exotic khichdi from Bengal – an appetizing, perfect combination of rice, masoor dal and mixed veggies. With loads of protein, fibre and iron and minimum fat, this one sure is a delectable way to lose weight.

25 mm. (1") stick cinnamon (*dalchini*)
2 cloves (*laung/ lavang*)
2 cardamom (*elaichi*)
1 tsp ghee
½ cup finely chopped onions
2 bayleaves (*tejpatta*)
2 tsp crushed garlic (*lehsun*)
2 tsp grated ginger (*adrak*)
1 cup uncooked brown rice / rice (*chawal*), washed, soaked and drained
¾ cup *masoor dal* (split red lentils), washed and drained
½ cup potato cubes
⅓ chopped French beans
½ cup fresh green peas
2 tsp finely chopped green chillies
½ tsp turmeric powder (*haldi*)
Salt to taste

For the garnish
A few ginger *(adrak)* strips

1. Combine the cinnamon, cloves and cardamom and coarsely ground them using a mortar-pestle (*khalbhatta*). Keep aside.
2. Heat the ghee in a deep non-stick pan, add the ground spices, onions, bayleaves, garlic and ginger, mix well and sauté on a medium flame for 2 to 3 minutes.
3. Add the rice, *masoor dal*, potatoes, French beans, green peas, green chillies and turmeric powder, mix well and sauté on a medium flame for another 2 minutes.
4. Add 4 cups of hot water and salt, mix well and cover and cook on a medium flame for 10 to 12 minutes, stirring occasionally.
5. Lower the flame and cook for another 10 to 12 minutes or till the vegetables are soft and the rice is cooked.
   Serve hot garnished with ginger strips.

Nutritive values per serving	
Energy	: 230 calories
Protein	**: 11.0 gm**
Carbohydrates	: 52.7 gm
Fat	: 1.7 gm
Iron	**: 2.8 mg**
Zinc	**: 1.5 mg**
Fibre	**: 1.0 gm**

Hare Lehsun ki Dal

Preparation Time: 10 minutes.   Cooking Time: 25 minutes.   Serves 4.
Soaking time: 15 minutes.

A mildly spiced dal, which goes well with rice, it is tasty, flavourful, healthy and nutritious. Replacing the traditional tempering of loads of ghee with a little oil, makes it an ideal addition to your weight loss menu.

¾ cup toovar (arhar) dal
¼ tsp turmeric powder (haldi)
Salt to taste
1 tsp oil
½ tsp cumin seeds (jeera)
2 whole dry Kashmiri red chillies, broken into pieces
½ tsp ginger-green chilli paste
¼ tsp asafoetida (hing)
⅓ cup finely chopped green garlic (hara lehsun)
¼ cup finely chopped tomatoes

For the garnish
2 tbsp finely chopped coriander (dhania)

1. Clean, wash and soak the dal in enough water for 15 minutes. Drain and keep aside.
2. Add the turmeric powder, salt and 3 cups of water, mix well and pressure cook for 3 whistles or till the dal is done.
3. Allow the steam to escape before opening the lid. Remove, whisk well and keep aside.
4. Heat the oil in a deep non-stick pan and add the cumin seeds.
5. When the seeds crackle, add the red chillies, ginger-green chilli paste, asafoetida and green garlic, mix well and sauté on a medium flame for 2 to 3 minutes.
6. Add the tomatoes and sauté on a medium flame till the oil separates form the mixture.
7. Add the dal and ½ cup of water and bring to boil.
Serve hot garnished with the coriander.

Nutritive values per serving

Energy	: 151 calories
Protein	**: 9.3 gm**
Carbohydrates	: 24.1 gm
Fat	: 2.0 gm
Vitamin A	**: 203.4 mcg**
Folic Acid	**: 45.6 mcg**
Fibre	**: 0.7 gm**

Suva Masoor Dal

Preparation Time: 10 minutes.   Cooking Time: 20 minutes.   Serves 4.
Soaking time: 15 minutes.

A perfect combination with steaming rice, this low-cal spicy dal is perfect to get back to pre-pregnancy shape. Dill leaves and garlic add flavour. Turmeric is a well-known anti-bacterial agent, while protein from masoor dal strengthens muscles, which become weak after delivery.

¾ cup *masoor dal* (split red lentil)
¼ tsp turmeric powder (*haldi*)
Salt to taste
1 tsp oil
½ tsp cumin seeds (*jeera*)
2 to 3 curry leaves (*kadi patta*)
2 tsp chopped garlic (*lehsun*)
½ tsp chopped green chillies
¼ cup finely chopped onions
2 tbsp finely chopped dill (*shepu /suva bhaji*) leaves

1. Clean, wash and soak the *dal* for about 15 minutes. Drain and keep aside.
2. Combine the *dal* with turmeric powder, salt and 1¼ cups of hot water in a pressure cooker and cook for at least 2 whistles.
3. Allow the steam to escape before opening the lid. Remove, whisk well and keep aside.
4. Heat the oil in a deep non-stick pan and add the cumin seeds.
5. When the seeds crackle, add the curry leaves, garlic, green chillies, onions and sauté till the onions turn light brown in colour.
6. Add the cooked *dal* and ½ cup of water and bring to boil.
7. Add the dill leaves, mix well and simmer for 5 to 7 minutes.
Serve hot.

Nutritive values per serving

Energy	: 81 calories
Protein	**: 4.9 gm**
Carbohydrates	: 12.2 gm
Fat	: 1.4 gm
Vitamin A	**: 170.3 mcg**
Iron	**: 1.8 mg**

Methiche Varan

Preparation Time: 20 minutes.   Cooking Time: 15 minutes.   Serves 4.
Soaking Time: 20 minutes.

Indulge in this low-cal but authentic Maharashtrian dal loaded with methi leaves – rich in fibre, folic acid, and iron. I have replaced sugar with jaggery which enhances the taste and the iron content.

1 cup *toovar* (*arhar*) *dal*, soaked for 20 minutes and drained
¼ tsp turmeric powder (*haldi*)
Salt to taste
2 tsp grated jaggery (*gur*), optional
½ tsp chilli powder
1 tsp ghee
¼ tsp asafoetida (*hing*)
4 to 5 cloves garlic (*lehsun*), crushed (*optional*)
1 cup finely chopped fenugreek (*methi*) leaves

1. Combine the *dal*, turmeric powder, salt and 3 cups of hot water in a pressure cooker and cook for 3 to 4 whistles or till the *dal* is done.
2. Allow the steam to escape before opening the lid.
3. Whisk well, add ½ cup of water, jaggery and chilli powder, mix well and bring to boil.
4. For the tempering, heat the ghee in a small non-stick pan, add the asafoetida and garlic and sauté on a medium flame till the garlic turns light brown in colour.
5. Add the fenugreek leaves and sauté on a medium flame for another 2 minutes.
6. Pour this tempering over the boiling *dal* and mix well.
   Serve hot.

Nutritive values per serving	
Energy	: 164 calories
Protein	: 9.5 gm
Carbohydrates	: 26.9 gm
Fat	: 2.0 gm
Iron	: 1.3 mg
Folic Acid	: 42.2 mcg
Fibre	: 0.7 gm

Dapka Kadhi

Preparation Time: 15 minutes. Cooking Time: 20 minutes. Serves 4.
Soaking time: 5 to 6 hours.

Kadhi lovers will enjoy this one - a yummy combination of non-fried moong dal dumplings and the traditional Gujarati kadhi. This dish is rich in protein – an essential aid to losing weight. Serving it with pulao or khichdi is a great way to increase the protein in your diet.

To be mixed together into a batter
1 cup yellow *moong dal* (split yellow gram), soaked for 5 to 6 hours and ground into a paste
1 tsp ginger-green chilli paste
½ tsp sugar
A pinch soda-bi-carb (optional)
Salt to taste

Other ingredients
2 tbsp *besan* (Bengal gram flour)
¾ cup fresh low-fat curds (*dahi*), page 94
1 tsp ginger-green chilli paste
6 to 8 curry leaves (*kadi patta*)
2 tsp sugar
Salt to taste
1 tsp ghee
½ tsp mustard seeds (*rai/sarson*)
½ tsp cumin seeds (*jeera*)
A pinch asafoetida (*hing*)
1 whole dry Kashmiri red chilli, broken into pieces
2 tbsp finely chopped coriander (*dhania*)

1. Combine the *besan*, curds and 4 cups of water in a bowl and whisk till smooth.
2. Add the ginger-green chilli paste, curry leaves, sugar and salt, mix well and put to boil.
3. Simmer on a medium flame for 5 to 7 minutes, while stirring occasionally.
4. Heat the ghee in a small non-stick pan and add the mustard seeds and cumin seeds.
5. When the seeds crackle, add the asafoetida and red chillies and sauté on a medium flame for a few seconds.
6. Add this tempering to the boiling *kadhi* and cover it immediately.
7. To the boiling *kadhi*, drop spoonfuls of the prepared *moong dal* batter and simmer for 5 to 7 minutes or till the *dapkas* are cooked and start floating.
8. Add the coriander, mix well and serve hot.

Handy tip: Ensure the *moong dal* batter is not very thick nor very thin. Add a spoonful of the batter to the boiling *kadhi* and wait for it to float up. If it does not float, it means the batter is too thin. You can add a little *besan* to the batter and proceed as per the recipe given above.

Nutritive values per serving	
Energy	: 184 calories
Protein	**: 11.4 gm**
Carbohydrates	: 30.0 gm
Fat	: 2.0 gm
Calcium	**: 87.1 mg**
Iron	**: 1.7 mg**
Zinc	**: 1.1 mg**

Subzi Kadhi

Preparation Time: a few minutes. **Cooking Time:** 15 minutes. **Serves 4.**

In my variation of the Gujarati kadhi, veggies add loads of vitamins, while the low amount of ghee keeps the calorie count down. Serve with khichdi or steaming hot rice to relish a complete meal. Avoid sour curds as it may not suit the new mother.

2 tbsp *besan* (Bengal gram flour)
1 cup fresh low-fat curds (*dahi*), page 94
1 tsp ginger-green chilli paste
2 curry leaves (*kadi patta*)
1 tbsp sugar
Salt to taste
1 tsp ghee
½ tsp cumin (*jeera*) seeds
½ tsp mustard seeds (*rai/sarson*)
A pinch asafoetida (*hing*)
1 whole dry Kashmiri red chilli, broken into pieces
1 cup chopped and boiled mixed vegetables (carrots, French beans and cauliflower)
1 tbsp chopped coriander (*dhania*)

1. Combine the *besan* and curds in a bowl and whisk well till smooth.
2. Add the green chilli-ginger paste, curry leaves, sugar, salt and 3 cups of water and keep aside.
3. Heat the ghee in a deep non-stick pan and add the cumin seeds and mustard seeds.
4. When the seeds crackle, add the asafoetida and red chillies and sauté on a medium flame for a few seconds.
5. Add the *besan*-curds mixture, mixed vegetables and coriander and bring to boil.
6. Lower the flame and simmer for 3 to 4 minutes. Serve hot.

Nutritive values per serving

Energy	: 87 calories
Protein	: 3.2 gm
Carbohydrates	: 14.8 gm
Fat	: 1.6 gm
Calcium	**: 96.3 mg**
Fibre	**: 0.5 gm**

Jeera Pepper Rasam

Preparation Time: 15 minutes. Cooking Time: 10 to 12 minutes. Serves 4.

Some times common cold and feverishness after pregnancy call for a hot and spicy antidote – this jeera-pepper rasam is ideal to keep the sniffles away. I've restricted the ghee to 1 tsp, so enjoy this weight loss friendly dish plain or mixed with rice.

For the *masala*
½ tsp ghee
1 tsp black peppercorns (*kalimirch*)
1½ tsp cumin seeds (*jeera*)
1½ tsp *toovar* (*arhar*) *dal*
1 whole dry Kashmiri red chilli, broken into pieces
¼ tsp asafoetida (*hing*)

Other ingredients
1 tsp ghee
1 tsp mustard seeds (*rai/sarson*)
½ tsp cumin seeds (*jeera*)
1 whole dry Kashmiri red chilli, broken into pieces
7 to 8 curry leaves (*kadi patta*)
3 tbsp tamarind (*imli*) pulp, mixed with 2 cups of water
Salt to taste

For the *masala*
1. Heat the ghee in a small non-stick pan, add all the ingredients and sauté on a slow flame for 4 to 5 minutes or till they release a pleasant aroma. Keep aside to cool.
2. Blend in a mixer to a fine powder and keep aside.

How to proceed
1. Heat the ghee in a deep non-stick pan and add the mustard seeds.
2. When the seeds crackle, add the cumin seeds, red chillies and curry leaves and sauté on a medium flame for a few seconds.
3. Add the tamarind water and salt, mix well and simmer for 7 to 8 minutes or till the raw smell of tamarind disappears.
4. Add the prepared *masala*, mix well and simmer for another 2 minutes.
   Serve hot.

Nutritive values per serving	
Energy	: 23 calories
Protein	: 0.4 gm
Carbohydrates	: 1.1 gm
Fat	: 1.9 gm

Desserts

Healthy Sheera

Preparation Time: 5 minutes.   Cooking Time: 10 minutes.   Serves 4.

This sheera is made with protein rich whole wheat flour, nachni flour and soya flour, while jaggery add iron. Since I have used only 2 tsp of ghee and 1 tsp of almonds, it is definitely guilt-free.

2 tbsp whole wheat flour (*gehun ka atta*)
2 tbsp red millet (*ragi / nachni*) flour
2 tbsp soya flour
8 tsp grated jaggery (*gur*)
½ tsp cardamom (*elaichi*) powder
2 tsp ghee

For the garnish
1 tsp sliced almonds (*badam*)

1. Boil 1½ cups of water in a broad non-stick pan, add the jaggery to it and simmer till it melts. Remove in a bowl and keep aside.
2. Heat the ghee in the same non-stick pan, add all the flours and sauté on a slow flame till they turn light brown in colour.
3. Add the jaggery, water and cardamom, mix well till no lumps remain and simmer for another 2 to 3 minutes, while stirring continuously. Serve hot garnished with almonds.

Nutritive values per serving	
Energy	: 125 calories
Protein	: 3.3 gm
Carbohydrates	: 18.2 gm
Fat	: 4.3 gm
Iron	: 1.3 mg
Calcium	: 41.3 mg

Rose Barfi

Preparation Time: 15 minutes.   Cooking Time: Nil.   Makes 8 small pieces.

A colourful sweet that is high in protein and calcium and low in calories. Relish this rose flavoured sweet nibblets without worrying about piling on the extra weight. The simplicity of preparation makes it even better!

¾ cup crumbled low-fat *paneer* (cottage cheese), page 95
3 tbsp crumbled low-fat *mava* (khoya), page 96
¾ tbsp sugar substitute
A few drops rose essence
2-3 drops red food colour
¼ tsp ghee for greasing

1. Combine all the ingredients except the red colour in a bowl, add 2 tbsp of water and knead it till the mixture becomes smooth. Add a tbsp of water if required.
2. Divide this mixture into 2 equal portions. Add red colour to one portion and mix well.
3. Spread the white mixture evenly on a greased *thali* and keep aside.
4. Spread the remaining pink coloured mixture evenly over the white coloured mixture. Refrigerate for at least 1 hour.
5. Just before serving cut into 8 small pieces. Serve chilled.

Nutritive values per piece

Energy	: 80 calories
Protein	**: 6.8 gm**
Carbohydrates	: 12.4 gm
Fat	: 0.3 gm
Vitamin A	**: 423.3 mcg**
Calcium	**: 284.4 mg**

Sugar-free Date Rolls

Preparation Time: 5 minutes.   **Cooking Time:** Nil.   **Makes 6 rolls.**

These date rolls use only the sweetness of dates to satiate sugar cravings for lactating mothers. Mixed nuts like almonds, pistachio and walnuts add both nutrition and crunch. Indulge in moderation, though, because dry fruits are heavy in calories.

½ tsp ghee
¾ cup deseeded and finely chopped black dates (*khajur*)
1 tbsp chopped almonds (*badam*)
1 tbsp chopped pistachios
1 tbsp chopped walnuts (*akhrot*)
2 tbsp lightly roasted poppy seeds (*khus-khus*) for coating

1. Heat the ghee in a small non-stick pan, add the dates and cook on a slow flame, while stirring continuously for 5 to 7 minutes or till they turn into a soft lump.
2. Remove from the flame, add the almonds, pistachios and walnuts and mix well.
3. Divide the mixture into 6 equal portions and shape each portion into a roll.
4. Coat each roll evenly with poppy seeds and refrigerate to set.
   Serve chilled.

Nutritive values per roll

Energy	: 81 calories.
Protein	: 1.9 gm
Carbohydrates	: 9.6 gm
Fat	: 3.8 gm
Calcium	**: 75.2 mg**
Fibre	**: 0.9 gm**

Oats and Orange Rabadi

Preparation Time: 15 minutes.   Cooking Time: 25 minutes.   Serves 4.

This rabadi is an unbelievably tastier and healthier version of the traditional high calorie sweet. Low-fat milk, mava, minimal amount of ghee and high fibre oats brings the calorie count down to only 72 per serving – enough reason to forget the original!

½ cup orange segments
1 tsp sugar
¼ tsp ghee
1½ tbsp quick cooking rolled oats
2 cups low-fat milk (99.7% fat-free, readily available in the market)
1 tsp sugar substitute
1 tbsp low-fat *mava* (*khoya*), page 96
1 tbsp skim milk powder
¼ tsp cornflour mixed with 2 tbsp low-fat milk (99.7% fat-free, readily available in the market)
2 tsp orange flavoured drink mix

For the garnish
1 tbsp orange segments

1. Heat a small non-stick pan, add the orange and sugar, mix well and cook on a medium flame for 2 to 3 minutes.
2. Remove from the flame, cool sightly and refrigerate to chill.
3. Heat the ghee in a non-stick pan, add the oats and sauté on a medium flame for few seconds.
4. Add the milk, sugar substitute and *mava*, mix well and simmer for 8 to 10 minutes.
5. Add the milk powder and cornflour paste, mix well and simmer for 5 to 7 minutes or till the mixture thickens, while stirring continuously.
6. Remove from the flame and keep aside to cool. Refrigerate to chill.
7. Add the orange drink mix and cooked orange segments to the chilled *rabadi* and mix well.
   Serve immediately garnished with orange segments.

Nutritive values per serving	
Energy	: 72 calories
Protein	: 5.1 gm
Carbohydrates	: 10.8 gm
Fat	: 0.8 gm
Calcium	: 206.6 mg

Poha Phirni

Preparation Time: 5 minutes. Cooking Time: 10 minutes. Serves 4.

Iron rich poha and calcium rich milk are the twin pillars of this cool, nourishing dessert. Topping each portion with ¼ cup of mixed chopped fruits like apple, orange and strawberry would enhance the fibre content and also adds a lot of colour.

¾ cup beaten rice (*poha*)
3 cups low-fat milk (99.7% fat-free, readily available in the market)
¼ cup sugar
1 tbsp cornflour dissolved in 2 tsp cold low-fat milk (99.7% fat-free, readily available in the market)
½ tsp cardamom (*elaichi*) powder

For the garnish
A few saffron strands (*kesar*)

1. Roast the beaten rice in a non-stick pan till crisp, while stirring continuously. Do not allow to discolour.
2. Remove from the flame, cool and grind it coarsely. Keep aside.
3. Boil the milk in another non-stick pan, add the sugar and roasted beaten rice and simmer for 3 to 4 minutes, while stirring continuously.
4. Add the cornflour-milk mixture and cardamom powder, mix well and simmer for another 2 to 3 minutes. Cool completely and refrigerate for at least 1 hour.

Serve chilled garnished with saffron strands.

Nutritive values per serving	
Energy	: 92 calories
Protein	: 6.2 gm
Carbohydrates	: 15.9 gm
Fat	: 0.4 gm
Calcium	**: 230.6 mg**
Iron	**: 1.6 mg**

Fruit Bowl with Vanilla Cream

Preparation Time: 15 minutes.   Cooking Time: 10 minutes.   Serves 4.

Go on and indulge in this fibre, vitamin and protein rich dessert which looks and tastes exotic. Here's loads of taste with lesser the calories to keep the inches away.

For vanilla cream
1 tbsp chopped agar-agar (unflavoured china grass)
1 cup low-fat milk (99.7% fat-free, readily available in the market)
¾ tsp sugar substitute
⅛ tsp vanilla essence

Other ingredients
1 cup pineapple scoops
1 cup muskmelon (*kharbooja*) scoops
1 cup chopped banana
1 cup chopped apples

For the vanilla cream
1. Combine the agar-agar and 1½ tbsp of water in a small bowl. Place it on a double boiler and simmer till it dissolves completely.
2. Meanwhile put the milk to boil.
3. Remove from the flame, add the agar-agar and sugar substitute and mix well.
4. Strain the mixture and keep aside for 2 to 3 minutes.
5. Add the vanilla essence, mix well and pour the mixture into a bowl and put to set in the refrigerator.

How to proceed
1. Combine all the fruits in a bowl and refrigerate to chill.
2. Just before serving, place equal quantities of fruits in 4 individual bowls and top each bowl with equal quantities of vanilla cream. Serve immediately.

Nutritive values per serving

Energy	: 163 calories
Protein	: 3.0 gm
Carbohydrates	: 36.6 gm
Fat	: 0.5 gm
Vitamin A	: 254.3 mcg
Vitamin C	: 31.5 mg
Fibre	: 0.9 gm

Anjeer Basundi

Preparation Time: 10 minutes.   Cooking Time: 15 minutes.   Serves 4.

This unique version of the traditional basundi uses naturally sweet figs and low-fat milk. Sugar substitute keeps the calorie count in check.

1½ cups finely chopped fresh figs *(anjeer)*
4 cups low-fat milk (99.7% fat-free, readily available in the market)
½ tsp lemon juice
1 tsp cornflour dissolved in 1 tbsp low-fat milk (99.7% fat-free, readily available in the market)
½ cup low-fat *mava* (khoya), page 96
½ tbsp sugar substitute

For the garnish
4 fresh fig (*anjeer*) slices

1. Refrigerate the fig pieces to chill.
2. Pour the milk into a broad non-stick pan and bring to boil.
3. Lower the flame and simmer on a medium flame for 2 to 3 minutes, while stirring continuously.
4. Add the lemon juice drop by drop to the milk stirring continuously. You will see tiny curdled particles, which are required for the grainy texture of *basundi* (Refer handy tip).
5. Add the cornflour mixture, *mava* and sugar substitute, mix well and simmer for another 2 minutes.
6. Cool and refrigerate for at least 1 hour.
7. Add the figs to the thickened milk and mix well.
   Serve chilled garnished with fig slices.

Handy tip: Do not add the lemon juice all at once, if you do so the milk may curdle completely, you will get bigger curdled particles, which is not desirable.

Nutritive values per serving	
Energy	: 118 calories
Protein	: 11.0 gm
Carbohydrates	: 17.8 gm
Fat	: 0.3 gm
Calcium	: 454.3 mg

Basic Recipes

Low-Fat Curds

Preparation Time: A few minutes.   Cooking Time: 1 minute.   Makes 5 cups.
Setting Time: 5 to 6 hours.

Calcium rich curd is a well-known source of bacteria that aid digestion – this low-fat version will help you lose weight while retaining the taste and nutrition. Ideal when used to prepare meals or as accompaniment to parathas! I have used it in recipes like Cottage Cheese and Dill Canapes, page 26, Hot Borscht, page 34, Citrus Salad, page 39, Dry Figs and Banana Smoothie, page 45, Dapka Kadhi, page 82 etc.

1 litre low-fat milk (99.7% fat-free, readily available in the market)
1 tbsp curds (*dahi*)

1. Warm the milk.
2. Add the curds, mix well and cover.
3. Keep aside until the curds set (approx. 5 to 6 hours).
4. During the cold climate, place inside a casserole or closed oven to set.

Variation : Low-Fat Hung Curds
To get 1 cup of hung low-fat curds, tie 2 cups of low-fat curds in a muslin cloth and hang it for ½ an hour. Remove from the cloth and use as required.

Nutritive values per cup
Energy	: 71 calories
Protein	: 7.1 gm
Carbohydrates	: 10.2 gm
Fat	: 0.2 gm

Low-Fat Paneer

Preparation Time: A few minutes.   Cooking Time: 6 to 8 minutes.
Makes 70 grams (approx. ½ cup).

Health conscious mothers who want to lose weight will definitely enjoy this low-fat, guilt-free version of yummy, calcium rich paneer. Try your hand with this recipe and enjoy delicacies like Stuffed Wheat Dosa, page 22, Nourishing Moong Soup, page 31, Paneer, Carrot and Bean Sprouts Paratha, page 60, Baby Corn Paneer Jalfrazie, page 66 etc.

3 cups low-fat milk (99.7% fat-free, readily available in the market)
1½ cups low-fat curds (*dahi*), page 94, beaten

1. Put the milk to boil in a broad non-stick pan. When it starts boiling, add the curds and mix well.
2. Remove from the heat and stir gently until the milk curdles.
3. Strain and tie the curdled milk in a muslin cloth. Hang for about half an hour to allow the whey to drain out.
   Use as required.

Nutritive values per for ½ cup

Energy	: 315 calories
Protein	: 31.5 gm
Carbohydrates	: 45.0 gm
Fat	: 0.9 gm

Low-Fat Mava (Khoya)

Preparation Time: 5 minutes.   Cooking Time: 15 minutes.   Makes 1½ cups.

High calorie mava is a key ingredient in several sweets – it adds richness, taste and an essential grainy texture. Here's a low-fat, healthy version made from skim (low-fat) milk powder, which retains all the taste, without making you feel guilty about relishing your favourite sweets like Rose Barfi, page 87, Oats and Orange Rabadi, page 89 and Anjeer Basundi, page 92.

1 cup skim milk powder

1. Combine the milk powder with 6 tsp of water in a bowl and make a hard dough.
2. Wrap the dough in a muslin cloth and place in a sieve.
3. Place this sieve on a pan of boiling water and cover it with a lid. Let it steam for 10 minutes.
4. Remove from the flame and keep aside to cool.
5. Remove the cloth and grate the dough using a grater.
   Use as required.

Nutritive values for ½ cup

Energy	: 248 calories
Protein	: 26.3 gm
Carbohydrates	: 35.4 gm
Fat	: 0.1 gm

57318